Alice EATS WONDERLAND

....

> AN IRREVERENT ANNOTATED COOKBOOK
> ADVENTURE IN WHICH A GLUTTONOUS
> ALICE DEVOURS MANY OF THE
> WONDERLAND CHARACTERS

by AUGUST A. IMHOLTZ, JR. AND ALISON TANNENBAUM

with original illustrations by A. E. K. Carr

A BAUMHOLTZ BOOK

APPLEWOOD BOOKS
CARLISLE, MASSACHUSETTS

Parts of the text in Chapter 7 appeared previously (entitled "Stuffed Dormouse")
in *Bandersnatch*, the newsletter of the Lewis Carroll Society,
Issue No. 111, April 2001, pp. 16—18.

ISBN 978-1-4290-9106-0

Thank you for purchasing an Applewood book.

Applewood reprints America's lively classics —
books from the past that are still of interest to
modern readers. For a free copy of our current
catalog, please write to Applewood Books,
P. O. Box 27, Carlisle, MA 01741.

www.awb.com

Book design by Barbara DaSilva

Manufactured in the U.S.A.

TABLE OF CONTENTS

....

Readers are cautioned that some of the recipes contained herein are not intended to be prepared and/or consumed by humans or other living vertebrates. Neither of the authors is a magirologist. The recipes contained herein are intended to be entertaining and educational.

The authors are not responsible for any physiological, psychological, political, or religious consequences that may occur as a result of preparing or ingesting the dishes described in this cookbook. Such effects may include, but are not limited to: gastroenteritis, disgust, Ehrlichia, leptospirosis, shigellosis, salmonellosis (or any other "-oses"), arachnophobia, St. Vitus' Dance, horror, religious conversion, anorexia, cachexia (and other assorted "-exias"), Addison's Disease, livor mortis, septicemia, Republicanism, speaking in tongues, radiation sickness, Alice in Wonderland Syndrome, botulism, trichotillomania, and death.

Readers are further warned that some of the recipes in this cookbook call for body parts of endangered and/or protected species, and/or animals whose importation and/or slaughter may be prohibited by federal or local law. Potential cooks should research thoroughly any exotic ingredients called for. The authors are not responsible for any legal consequences that result from readers' disregard of this advice. Such scofflaws may be subject (at least) to federal or local prosecution, or (at worst), to some unspecified and unpredictable act of revenge on the part of Mother Nature. Do not attempt to contact the authors or the illustrator for assistance in making bail. (They can't afford it, anyway.)

AUTHORS' NOTES

About the story:

This cookbook adventure is based on Lewis Carroll's masterpiece, *Alice's Adventures in Wonderland*. The cookbook contains one or more excerpts from each of the twelve chapters of the original story, but each has been given a new twist, with the theme that Alice, like most children, is more or less constantly hungry. Her appetite is assuaged only by her pursuit of the animal characters (and some of the vegetables) that appear in the story. Alice learns to prepare, cook, and consume these, with the help of the included recipes. Although many of the characters seem, alas, to be transformed into edible dishes during the adventure, the story has a surprisingly happy ending. (With respect to the chapter headings, the authors apologize to Howard Roger Garis, author of the *Uncle Wiggily* series.)

About the annotations:

The notes that accompany each chapter of the story are intended to provide the reader with some of the natural and social history of the animals, food ingredients, and culture involved in aspects of the story. The authors have attempted to be as scientifically and academically correct as possible; the statements made in the notes are supported by the reliable sources provided in the reference section.

About the recipes:

In each chapter of the cookbook adventure, interesting and relevant recipes have been included; their sources are provided in the reference section. Some are intended to be followed; others are not. Hopefully, the reader will be able to tell the difference. The format, spelling, and ingredient names in the historic and/or culturally distinctive recipes have been retained wherever possible. Unfamiliar ingredients and terms may be described in the glossary (or, they may not). In the more modern recipes, spelling has been Americanized. Units of measure are given according to American standards, using the abbreviations "tsp." for a teaspoon measure, and "tbs." for a tablespoon measure. All other units of measure are spelled out. Oven temperatures are given in degrees Fahrenheit, although a table of conversions from Fahrenheit to GasMark is provided for our British reader.

About the illustrations:

The signed illustrations by A.E.K. Carr are original, created especially for this book, and have not been published previously. Sources for the other illustrations are given in the reference section.

About the glossary:

Definitions were compiled by the authors with the help of the *American Heritage Dictionary*, the *Oxford English Dictionary*, online and other encyclopedias, informational websites such as Wikipedia, their own specialized areas of knowledge, and their own lamentable imaginations.

The authors'

DEDICATION

....

For Mithaecus,
Greek author of the first known
Western cookbook, fifth century B.C.

Only one of his recipes survives, which is probably more than the number that should survive from this book.

Unfortunately, we do not have a picture of how Mithaecus' kitchen was appointed. However, the kitchen of his Renaissance follower, Marx Rumpolt, shown here, may resemble what Alice saw of the Dutchess' kitchen.[2]

Alice
EATS
WONDERLAND

ORANGES

"Oranges were originally cultivated in China and their history has been traced back some 20 million years, when the islands of the South Pacific were still part of the land mass that included Asia and Australia. It is believed that modern oranges [3] were developed from a bitter ancestral plant whose sacred seed was stolen from a Buddhist temple.

Arab traders brought the bitter orange, *Citrus aurantium*, from the east and cultivated it in the Mediterranean regions. The Moors introduced it to Spain, where it established itself and became known as the Seville orange. This is the orange used for making marmalade. Later the Crusaders brought oranges to northern Europe and while the climate was too cold for cultivation, it became the rage for royalty and the aristocracy to build orangeries in which to show off the trees and their fruit. One of the most lavish of such orangeries is at the Palace of Versailles, outside of Paris." [4]

CHAPTER 1, in which Alice learns the history of marmalade, encounters Marmite ™ soldiers, and prepares black pudding.

Oranges and lemons were first shipped to the UK from Spain in the thirteenth century as whole fruit, or as fruit and peel preserved in sugar syrup. At that time, oranges were still used for medicinal purposes, and were believed to promote "good appetite." [5]

The Renaissance painters believed that the orange had originated in Palestine and often included oranges and orange trees in their religious paintings. The significant and symbolic "Golden Apples of Hesperides" was one of these paintings. Oranges were included in "The Last Supper" and other works. Oranges and orange trees were considered symbols of the Virgin and were considered to represent love and fidelity.

"Alice was beginning to get very tired of sitting by her sister on the bank, and of having nothing to do…when suddenly a White Rabbit with pink eyes ran close by her…Burning with curiosity, she ran across the field after it, and fortunately was just in time to see it pop down a large rabbit-hole under the hedge. In another moment down went Alice after it, never once considering how in the world she was to get out again. The rabbit-hole went straight on like a tunnel for some way, and then dipped suddenly down, so suddenly that Alice had not a moment to think about stopping herself before she found herself falling down a very deep well.

Down, down, down. Would the fall NEVER come to an end!"

Alice had passed numerous familiar things on the way down — cupboards and bookshelves, and maps and pictures, and, of all things, an *empty* jar of marmalade! This was disappointing, as her long fall had made her ravenous, and she was very partial to toast with orange marmalade. She was so hungry that she temporarily abandoned her pursuit of the odd, pink-eyed white rabbit with the pocket watch to run home and get a snack.

French brides often refused to marry if they could not find orange blossoms to carry or wear. In Germany, oranges played an important role in dating since young girls often threw oranges from their balconies to encourage their suitors. Orange peels were used to redden lips long before lipstick was invented and they were purported to be a nostrum to banish evil thoughts from a woman's mind.

During Columbus' second voyage in 1493 he brought the first sweet orange seeds to the New World. The first planting of oranges and other citrus took place in Hispaniola. Ponce de Leon brought seedlings of orange trees, and while he never did find the Fountain of Youth, his contributions live on and have a profound effect on our diets. Some might even claim that orange juice (although only FLORIDA orange juice) represents the true Fountain of Youth.

"The first orange groves were established in Florida between 1513 and 1565 in and around the settlement of St. Augustine and along the St. Johns River. Assisted by Spanish explorers, missionaries and the Indians, sweet orange groves spread rapidly throughout the state."[6]

It is interesting to note that the first "marmalade" was actually made of quinces (not citrus fruit), when the Romans accidentally discovered the process of making a jelly. "They had traditionally preserved fruits in honey, but found that quinces weren't suitable for being preserved in this way, so they precooked the quinces in wine before adding the honey. This caused pectin to be released and the mixture set to form a quince jelly."[7]

SEVILLE orange marmalade

1 1/2 pounds Seville oranges
juice of 1 large lemon
1 1/2 cups water
3 pounds sugar, warmed

Wash the fruit, then cut it in half and squeeze out the juice. Tie the pith and pips in a muslin bag and shred the peel. Soak the peel and the muslin bag in the water overnight.

Put the peel, muslin bag, and the water in the pressure cooker. Put on the lid and bring to HIGH (15 pounds) pressure. Cook for 10 to 15 minutes, according to the thickness of the peel. Reduce pressure at room temperature. The peel must be really tender before the sugar is added. To test, let it cool, then press a piece of peel between thumb and forefinger.

When it is cool enough to handle, take out the muslin bag and squeeze the juice from it into the cooker. Then add the warmed sugar. Stir over gentle heat until the sugar is dissolved; then boil it rapidly in the open cooker until setting point is reached (sugar temperature should be 221°F.). Skim if necessary and let the marmalade cool until skin starts to form before pouring it into warm, dry jars. This prevents the peel rising in the jar. Cover each jar immediately with a waxed disc; when it is cool, cover with cellophane or a lid.

Yield: about 5 pounds marmalade [8]

MARMITE

While marmalade was often the spread of choice by the British for their cold, "racked" toast, there were times when the marmalade jar was empty, just like the ones Alice saw on her descent down the rabbit hole. In this situation, another popular choice for a bread spread was a brown, glutinous, vegetarian, odiferous preparation called Marmite™[10]. The name for this spread originated from the earthenware French cooking pot of the same name, which is shaped somewhat like the Marmite™ jar itself. The name of the French pot is pronounced "mar-MEET", and is named for the famous French soup, *petite marmite* (also called *pot au feu*), which is made from beef, chicken, and vegetables, and garnished with crisp toast rounds topped with melted Gruyere cheese and marrow from the beef bones.

"Marmite™ is a dark brown-colored savory spread made from the yeast that is a by-product of the brewing industry. It has a very strong, slightly salty flavor. It comes in a small (two to five inches high) bulb-shaped glass jar with a distinctive yellow lid. Children in Britain are generally fed it from the time they are weaned, and most never grow out of it. It has a high B-vitamin content, as well as riboflavin and niacin, and as such is very healthy. (The vitamin-B complex helps prevent anemia.)"[11]

"The basic raw material used in the manufacture of Marmite™ spread is spent brewer's yeast, a substance whose original and only use was to ferment sugars into alcohol. For many years this by-product of the brewing process was seen as a nuisance rather than a potentially valuable food source. In 1680 a Dutch scientist, Leouwanhoek, examined the yeast under a microscope and saw that it was composed of tiny spherical and ovoid cells. The French scientist Louis Pasteur realised that these cells were in fact living plants. Further investigation by a German chemist, Liebig, found that this yeast could be made into a concentrated food product which resembled meat extract in appearance, smell and colour, however it was vegetarian."[12]

A popular British breakfast item is "Marmite™ soldiers;" this consists of buttered toast, to which Marmite™ is applied. The toast is then cut into thin strips, or "soldiers."[13]

BATS AND CATS

As most readers will not be interested in learning of the gastronomical potential of bats (of any variety), and as some would certainly be offended by the thought of ingesting any part of a cat, we will not delve into menu possibilities for either of these mammalian groups.

> "...'do cats eat bats, I wonder?' And here Alice began to get rather sleepy, and went on saying to herself, in a dreamy sort of way, 'Do cats eat bats? Do cats eat bats?' and sometimes, 'Do bats eat cats?' for, you see, as she couldn't answer either question, it didn't much matter which way she put it."

Alice, who was quite hungry from the exertion of tumbling down the rabbit hole, thought the idea of either animal eating the other quite unpleasant. However, these gruesome questions did nothing to diminish her appetite, and she looked around to see if there was anything edible nearby.

> "Soon her eye fell on a little glass box that was lying under the table: she opened it, and found in it a very small cake, on which the words 'EAT ME' were beautifully marked in currants...So she set to work, and very soon finished off the cake." It was so delicious that she decided she would make some currant cakes herself...

Currants, however, are another story, as eating them is unlikely to be controversial. However, what is meant by the word *currant* can certainly be confusing, as that name is used interchangeably to refer to the fresh fruit of one group of plants, and to the dried fruit of another, unrelated, plant.

The currants that are used in their fresh form for jams, jellies, and desserts (shown here) are the fruit of fast-growing berry-producing deciduous shrubs of the botanical family Saxifragaceae. Red, pink, and white currants belong to three European species (*Ribes rubrum*, *Ribes petraeum*, *Ribes sativum*), respectively. Black currants are related to European (*Ribes nigrum* and *Ribes uva-crispa*) and Asian (*Ribes ussuriense*) species, but are less favored as a crop in North America because of their severe susceptibility to white pine blister rust. Currants thrive in temperate climates and have been grown in the United States since colonial times; they contain several minerals and are high in phosphorus and iron, and in vitamins A, B, and C. Currants have also been used for wine, and black currants are the traditional source of the French liqueur, Cassis. These plants were long referred to by their generic name, *Ribes*, which is of ancient Indo-European origin and is common to other languages. The English word *currant* has been used for this fruit only since 1550, and hence is the source of the confusion between the fresh fruit and the dried currants favored by the British as a flavorful addition to their tea-time scones and pastries.[14] Adoption of the English word *currant* for the fresh fruit was based on its resemblance to the small raisins of Greece. (A graphic lesson in the value of using botanical, rather than common, names for plants!)

Dried currants [15] are a type of very small raisin (of the botanical family Vitaceae) made from the Black Corinth grape (sold fresh as "Champagne grapes"). They are seedless and very dark in color. The flavor of dried currants is reminiscent of raisins but they have a lighter flavor and something of an anise undertone. About one-fourth the size of other raisins, dried currants are sometimes labeled "Zante Currants," referring to the Greek island where the Black Corinth grapes first grew. The name *currant* is probably a corruption of the word *Corinth*,[16] the location from which currants were shipped across the ancient world. Dried currants, like other raisins, are a concentrated source of calories, sugar, and nutrients. They also supply dietary fiber (both soluble and insoluble), as well as some iron, potassium, and B and C vitamins.

The first raisins were most likely grapes that had dried naturally on the vine. The human practice of picking grapes and laying them in the sun to dry dates back at least three thousand years, and this process has remained virtually unchanged. Raisins were a valued trade item in the ancient Near East and also highly valued in ancient Rome, where two jars of raisins could be exchanged for a slave.[17] Spanish missionaries brought them to Mexico and California in the eighteenth century, and nearly all the commercially grown raisins in the United States (and about one-half of the total world supply) now come from the San Joaquin valley of California, where the raisin industry began booming in 1873 after a heat wave serendipitously dried the grape crop on the vine.[18]

---

victorian currant cakes

1 cup currants

1/2 cup brandy

1/2 pound butter

1 heaping cup granulated sugar

1 whole egg

1 egg yolk

1/2 tsp. ground nutmeg

1/2 tsp. ground cinnamon

2 1/2 to 2 3/4 cups flour, sifted

Soak currants in brandy for 30 minutes; drain and reserve brandy.

Cream butter and sugar until light and fluffy.

Add egg, egg yolk, and spices, and mix well.

Add 2 tsp. of the reserved brandy, and the currants, and mix.

Add enough flour to make a smooth, but light, dough.

Wrap dough in waxed paper and chill for 1 hour.

Pinch off small pieces of dough and arrange on a greased cookie sheet about 2 inches apart.

Flatten with a fork.

Bake at 350°F for about 10 minutes.

Remove to wire racks to cool; store in airtight container.[19]

As Alice was preparing the currant cakes, she nicked her finger with a knife. She had been taught that *"if you cut your finger VERY deeply with a knife, it usually bleeds; and she had never forgotten that."*

This brought to Alice's little mind, by that curious form of association typical of deans' daughters, the recipe her grandmother had used for blood pudding...

Collecting blood for food use during butchering[20]

ANIMAL BLOOD

In virtually all cultures, on every continent, animal blood, a source of high-quality nutrition, is, or was, ingested by humans as a normal part of their diet. Doing so helped to conserve the by-products of animals raised for meat, and eliminated the waste of valuable resources that were expended in raising the animals for slaughter. Blood was often made into sausages, used in meat dishes along with organ or muscle meat from the same or a different species, or mixed with milk and ingested fresh (e.g., by the Masai of Africa), or cooked.

BLACK PUDDING

1 pint fresh pig's blood

4 ounces pearl barley, rice, or groats

4 ounces fine oatmeal

1 ounce salt

1/4 tsp. pepper

1/2 pound diced beef suet or fat

2 ounces finely chopped or minced onions

Cook the barley, rice, or groats in four times its volume of water until just soft. Mix the oatmeal with salt and pepper and stir to a paste with a little strained blood. Add the cereal, suet or fat, onions, and the remaining strained blood to the mixture. Put into [sausage] skins through a funnel, stirring the mixture frequently to prevent the fat separating out. Alternatively, put the mixture into a greased baking tin and bake in the oven at 350°F for 45 minutes.

Tie the sausage skins loosely and drop into hot, but not boiling, water; the addition of black pudding dye will ensure an attractive dark finish. Boil for 20 minutes or until no blood comes out when a pudding is pricked with a needle. To serve, heat the puddings through in hot water for 10 to 15 minutes, or score at intervals and grill for 4 minutes on each side.

Alternatively, cut into rounds and grill or fry in lard. Serve with eggs for breakfast or with a mixed grill for lunch or high tea. In Derbyshire and Staffordshire, black pudding slices are served on oatcakes with fried eggs on top.[21]

WELSH RABBIT

For those readers who are squeamish, or have moral, ethical, misophobic, microbiophobic, or spermatophobic objections to preparing or ingesting the meat of rabbits, we will begin our discussion of rabbits with a "rabbit" dish that does not require the use of a rabbit at all: Welsh rabbit. This nutritious meal contains no meat whatsoever. Eighteenth-century English cookbooks recommend Welsh rabbit as a supper or tavern dish. It is based on the fine cheddar-type cheeses and the wheat breads that were central to English cuisine. Surprisingly, there were not only a Welsh (or Welch) rabbit, but also an English rabbit, an Irish, and a Scotch rabbit. By the late nineteenth century, the dish had achieved elevated status as "rarebit," and was served more elegantly, in chafing dishes.

The Columbia Guide to Standard American English simplifies the concept: "*Welsh rabbit* and *Welsh rarebit* are both Standard English names for a dish of melted cheese and beer served on toast or crackers, presumably so called as an insult to the impoverished or uncivilized Welsh, who were said to eat it

> CHAPTER 2, in which Alice encounters rabbits made of cheese, learns to dress a rabbit, and prepares a mumble of rabbit.

instead of the rabbit meat they lacked; hence *Welsh rabbit* is almost certainly an ethnic slur. *Welsh rarebit* is a folk etymology apparently either contrived to avoid offending the Welsh or caused by a misunderstanding of the intended noun, since perhaps some couldn't see a connection between cheese and rabbits."[22]

"After a time she heard a little pattering of feet in the distance, and she hastily dried her eyes to see what was coming. It was the White Rabbit returning, splendidly dressed, with a pair of white kid gloves in one hand and a large fan in the other..."

A rabbit being "dressed" in items of clothing reminded Alice that the word "dressed" had another meaning, as in being prepared for cooking. She had become very hungry, and thought that a rabbit dish would be delicious right about now. Because she had no immediate idea of how to "dress" (second meaning) a rabbit, she decided first to make a simple dish called Welsh Rabbit, which did not require an actual rabbit, but would serve her immediate purpose just as well.

WELCH RABBIT

Cut a handſome Piece of Bread and an even Slice of Cheeſe, let the Bread be of the Shape of the Cheeſe, put a little larger every Way. Put a salamander in the Fire, or a large Poker, or the Bottom of a Fire-Shovel heated red hot will do.[24]

SCOTCH RABBIT

Cut a Slice of Cheeſe very large and handſome, cut a Slice of Bread, without Cruſt, juſt of the Size of the Cheeſe; I toaſt the Bread an both Sides, and butter it, then toaſt the Cheeſe on both Sides, and lay it evenly upon the Toaſt and Butter. Send it up hot without Muſtard. This ſhould be made larger than the Welch Rabbit, and ſent up ſingle, one in a Plate, as that ſhould be two.[25]

ENGLIFH RABBIT

Cut a handſome Toaſt of Bread without Cruſt, and have a good Quantity Cheeſe very fine. Set a Tin Oven before the Fire, and have in Readineſs a Glaſs of red Port Wine.
Toaſt the Bread carefully on both Sides, then pour the Wine upon it, and turn it.
When it has ſoaked up the Wine ſpread the ſcraped Cheeſe thick upon it, lay it in the Oven, and place it before a good Fire; the Cheeſe will do very quickly and very finely.[26]

MODErn WELSH RABBIT WITH BEEr

I tbs. butter	I tsp. dry mustard
I pound sharp cheddar cheese, grated	1/2 tsp. salt
	1/2 tsp. Worcestershire sauce
3/4 cup beer	I egg, slightly beaten
Dash cayenne pepper or Tabasco sauce	8 slices warm toast, halved

In the top of a double boiler set over hot (not boiling) water, melt butter. Add cheese and all but I tbs. of the beer. Cook, stirring constantly, until cheese has melted and the mixture is smooth. Combine seasonings with remaining beer and stir into cheese. Beat a little of the hot mixture into the beaten egg to prevent curdling before adding the egg mixture to the melted cheese. Stir to combine. Arrange 4 triangles of toast on each plate and top each immediately with 1/4 of the rabbit.[27]

Mrs. Martha Bradley's directions for "rabbit" specified "Bread crisp and soft."[23] The crisp toast was arranged on a plate or platter, sometimes with crusts removed, sometimes buttered, and sometimes sprinkled with ale or wine. Over this was arranged the cheese or cheese mixture.

The cheese (traditionally, Cheshire cheese) could be slivered and melted separately (often with the addition of beer or mustard), or simply cut as a slab and placed on the toast. Either method required a final heating with a hot instrument. According to Mrs. Bradley, "Put a Salamander in the Fire, or a large Poker, or the Bottom of a Fire-Shovel heated red hot will do." A salamander is a thick plate of iron attached to a long handle with two feet, or rests, arranged near the heavy end for propping into the heat. Its purpose was to absorb and hold a substantial quantity of heat so that when it was passed, glowing red, over a dish such as Welsh rabbit, it would broil it quickly. Its name apparently refers to a woodland amphibian that, according to ancient legend, could survive a fire and return to life, phoenix-like. For these recipes, substitute a broiler or toaster oven for the "salamander."

As can be seen from the small sample of recipes to the left, there are many versions of Welsh rabbit.

When Alice had finished off the Welsh Rarebit, and she had replenished her energy, she was ready to take on the task of preparing a *real* rabbit dish…

RABBIT

Rabbits (which are lagomorphs, not rodents!) are indigenous to many areas of the world, and have been introduced to many others. They have been used for human food since at least 1500 B.C. Sailing vessels distributed rabbits on islands in various sea lanes to reproduce and be used as a source of food by sailors on subsequent voyages.

Rabbits [28] have been domesticated in many cultures, but wild rabbits are often hunted and eaten, too. Rabbit meat is currently underutilized as a meat source, which is surprising, given that rabbit meat is all white meat, has the fewest calories per pound, and is higher in protein and lower in fat than any other domestic meat. In fact, the United States Office of Home Economics has done extensive testing of the nutritive values of many meats, and goes so far as to state that "domestic rabbit meat is the most nutritious meat known to man." [29]

In order to prepare rabbit dishes, it might well be necessary, as Alice found, to "dress" the rabbit first. Should a reader have occasion to need it, here is the procedure recommended by both the Virginia and Mississippi State Extension Services. [30]

(We will not address here how the rabbit should be incapacitated and/or done in. Note, however, on this subject, that the United States Department of Agriculture warns that carcasses from animals killed by electrocution should not be processed for food.)

a. Wear rubber gloves when preparing wild rabbits; they may carry tularemia, a disease that can be transmitted to humans.

b. Wash the rabbit and eviscerate it as soon as possible.

    1. Check for scent glands under the front legs and dissect them out carefully, or they will impart an unpleasant flavor to the meat.

    2. Avoid cutting into the viscera, as this will have a similar effect.

    3. Examine the liver for encysted parasites; if none is present, and the liver is a good dark reddish-brown color, the rabbit probably does not have tularemia. Otherwise, discard the rabbit.

c. Cut off the head, feet and tail. The feet can be saved and used as "good luck" icons for keychains. (They weren't very lucky for the rabbit, though.) We offer no suggestions for the use of the head, and leave that to the reader's imagination.

d. Rinse the carcass well in cold water.

e. Cut the animal into serving size pieces. The following diagram and step-wise notes may be helpful.

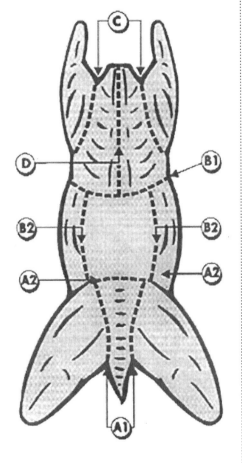

A. Remove rear legs and tail. Cut parallel to and on each side of tail forward until knife contacts the leg bones.

    1. Cut perpendicular to spine in front of hip joint on each leg.

    2. Remove each leg by twisting to separate the joint.

    3. Cut through spine to remove tail.

B. Remove back and flanks.

    1. Cut across at level of shoulders.

    2. Cut through spine and along ribs.

    3. Remove flanks by separating each flank from the back.

C. Remove front legs.

D. Split the rib cage with a cleaver or large knife.

Rabbit Pie

1 rabbit	1/2 tsp. of grated nutmeg
a few slices of ham	forcemeat
salt	3 hard-boiled eggs
white pepper	1/2 pint of gravy
2 blades of pounded mace	1/2 pound of puff paste

Cut up the rabbit *[see diagram]* (which should be young), remove the breastbone, and bone the legs. Put the rabbit, slices of ham, forcemeat balls, and hard-boiled eggs in layers, and season each layer with pepper, salt, pounded mace, and ground nutmeg. Pour in about 1/2 pint of water, cover with puff paste, and bake in a moderate oven for about 1 1/2 hours. Should the crust acquire too much color, place a piece of paper over it to prevent its burning. When done, pour in at the top, by means of the hole in the middle of the crust, a little good gravy made of the breast and leg bones of the rabbit and 2 or 3 shin bones of beef, flavored with onion, herbs, and spices. Note: the liver of the rabbit may be boiled, minced, and mixed with the forcemeat if the flavor is liked.[31]

Mumbled Rabbit

This nineteenth-century procedure is recommended for older, tougher rabbits.

Clean, skin, and fill bellies with parsley and onions whole, and stew them till the meat falls from the bones (which pick out). Chop up the meat, onions, and parsley and meanwhile thicken the gravy in the pot with flour and butter, and season with pepper, spice and cider, return the chopped meat and onions into this thick sauce to reheat. Serve on snippets of fried toast. Mushrooms or old garden peas may be added to the "mumble." If cider is not available, use sour apples or a small spoonful of vinegar while stewing.[32]

One additional rabbit dish in which the reader might be interested is "Rillettes of Rabbit," a sort of paté included in a "multisensory" experimental menu for "The Mad Hatter's Dinner Party," conceived by Paul Clayton, Helen Conn, and Heston Blumenthal: "The rabbit confit is cooked for about two days with white wine and rosemary, duck and fois gras fat, then the meat shredded in reduced rabbit juices."[33]

In medieval times, those who maintained strict observance of the numerous fast days and the entire forty days of Lent missed meat tremendously. The rules set out in the guidelines for the Catholic faith during the Middle Ages stated that animals from the sea could appropriately be used as food during such fast periods. The key requirement was that the species eaten must live in water, but the animal kingdom to which they belonged was not specified. It is by this questionable logic that fetal animals (those immersed in "water," or amniotic fluid; e.g., veal) were permitted for meatless days. Further convenient extrapolations of the rules were made, including two reported by Gerald of Wales, in the twelfth century. He observed that monks consumed beaver tails on fast days because they were held to be fish, according to *Topographia Hiberniae* and the *Itinerarium Kambriae* (which refer to Pliny's *Historia Naturalis*).[34] He also reported that barnacle geese were believed to grow on trees in Ireland, and that they could be eaten on fast days because they were not "flesh." These exceptions were extended into another "rule" (whether official or unofficial) made by monks in certain monasteries that some additional types of "white" animal flesh would not count as meat during Lent. Among these was rabbit meat. Go figure.

DODO

The gray, or common, dodo was first sighted on its native Mauritius sometime between 1507 and 1598 (accounts vary), when Portuguese and Dutch sailors landed there. Sources do agree, though, that the turkey-sized flightless bird we know as the dodo (*Raphus cucullatus*; formerly *Didus ineptus*; family, Raphidae; order, Columbiformes, a family perhaps better known for another member, the common pigeon; see also DNA evidence, cited below) was extinct eighty to one hundred years later, and certainly by 1681. [35]

Because humans were previously unknown on the island, and because the large birds apparently had no predators, they showed no fear of man, and thus were named "dodo," either from the Portuguese "duodo," a simpleton, or from the Dutch "dodoor," a sluggard. [36]

Dodos were large gray birds with short yellow legs and a large, hooked bill. Their wings, tail, breastbone, and pectoral

CHAPTER 3, in which Alice constructs a DoDuckMus, quiets bickering crabs, and prepares spindled oysters.

muscles were underdeveloped, and the birds were not capable of flight. Dodos have traditionally been depicted as plump and slow, but recent evidence suggests that early portraits of the birds [37] were based on captive specimens that were well-fed and inactive, and indicates that the wild bird probably weighed in the range of thirteen to seventeen kilograms, rather than earlier estimates of twenty to twenty-three kilograms. The one existing dodo skeleton consists of bones from several different individuals; there exists no complete specimen. [38]

"They were indeed a queer-looking party that assembled on the bank — the birds with draggled feathers, the animals with their fur clinging close to them, and all dripping wet, cross, and uncomfortable…"

Alice had found her time in the pool of tears stressful and exhausting. She felt that the mouse's tale was tiresome, and was aggravated by the other animals' whining. Her thoughts naturally turned to food. The dodo would certainly provide a delicious meal (if she could figure out how to subdue it), and she loved roast duck! She wondered, too, how a mouse would taste (although she did not let on to the mouse that she was thinking in this direction)… She had heard of an elegant poultry dish called TurDuckEn, which consisted of a stuffed boned chicken inside a boned duck, inside a boned turkey, all roasted together. It would be a little complicated, but perhaps she could do something similar with the species at hand, the dodo, the duck, and the mouse, and perhaps create a DoDuckMus?

"Dr Andrew Kitchener has created two life-size reproductions of the dodo — one is housed in the Royal Museum of Scotland in Edinburgh and the other is in the University Museum, Oxford. They are based on research using hundreds of actual [partial] dodo skeletons and bones unearthed by naturalists in the Mare aux Songes swamp in South-east Mauritius... Dr Kitchener's research presents us with a lithe, active, smart dodo superbly adapted to live and survive prosperously in the forests of its native Mauritius... In 1991, further credence was given to this new image of the dodo, when a series of long-lost drawings by

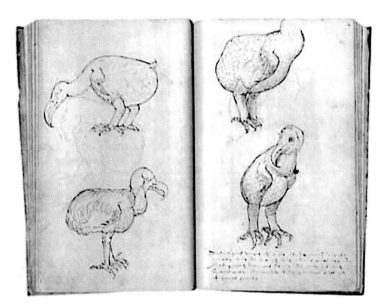

Harmanszoon dating from 1601 (shown here) were discovered in The Hague after having been lost for over 150 years."[39, 40]

While some dodos were taken on board ship, and perhaps kept alive on deck for some months as a source of fresh meat, the Dutch killed far more of them in hunting expeditions, even though "they apparently found the meat exceedingly tough no matter how long it was boiled."[41] However, the primary causes of the dodo's demise and extinction were destruction of their forest habitat and

predation by introduced species (such as dogs, pigs, and monkeys) left on the island by sailors. These animals became feral and multiplied rapidly on the isolated island. They (along with feral ship rats) found dodo eggs and young easy prey, because dodos nested on the ground, and laid a single egg in a nest made of grasses.[42]

Scientists believe that the dodo evolved from an ancestor capable of flight, probably migratory African pigeons whose navigation was deficient and who landed on, and colonized, Mauritius. There, the dodo's ancestors found a habitat with abundant food (indigenous fruits that fell to the ground when ripe) and no predators. The dodo's ancestors separated from their closest pigeon relatives some twenty-five million years ago, and the dodo eventually evolved into a terrestrial bird. Because flying requires a high expenditure of energy, it was physiologically more efficient for the dodo to remain on the ground and store fat (that could be utilized at times when the food supply was poor) than to fly.

Recent molecular analysis of DNA retrieved from a dodo specimen at the Oxford University Museum of Natural History (England), confirms that the bird belongs firmly in the middle of the pigeon tree in evolutionary terms.[43] The dodo's closest living relative is the Nicobar pigeon, of the Nicobar Islands and other parts of Southeast Asia; it was primarily a ground-dweller.

DUCKS

Much has been written on the culinary uses and fine gustatory properties of both the wild [44] and domestic duck of the genera *Aix* and *Anas*, and thus we need not go into that here, except to remind readers that except for the larger Muscovy duck (*Cairina moschata*, originally from Brazil), all strains of domestic duck are derived from the wild mallard, *Anas platyrhyncos*. It is interesting to note that domestic ducks, bred for large body size and high proportion of meat, resemble the dodo in that they cannot fly.

TURDUCKEN

Skin and bone a chicken and a duck, and bone a turkey, being careful to work from the inside and not damage the outsides of any of the fowl. Stuff the chicken with your favorite stuffing, season with salt and pepper, and insert the chicken into the cavity of the duck. Fill in any empty spaces in the duck with more stuffing. Season the duck, and insert the duck into the cavity of the turkey, again filling any gaps with stuffing. Close the ends of the turkey with its own skin, season with salt and pepper, and bake at 350° for 20 minutes per pound of the turkey, or until a fork inserted deep into the TurDuckEn releases no blood. Let rest for 15 minutes. To serve, slice crosswise so that all the layers may be appreciated.[45]

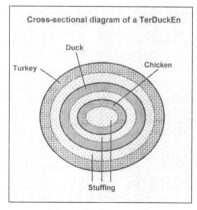

Schematic diagram of a completed TurDuckEn

The animals continued to be grumpy, and gripe among themselves, and Alice observed that "...*an old Crab took the opportunity of saying to her daughter 'Ah, my dear! Let this be a lesson to you never to lose YOUR temper!' 'Hold your tongue, Ma!' said the young Crab, a little snappishly. 'You're enough to try the patience of an oyster!' "*

Although she was a little tired after the ordeal of constructing the DoDuckMus, Alice still found the idea of a dish made with crabs and/or oysters appealing, especially since it would diminish the aggravation of having to listen to the crabs' bickering.

MICE

Preparation of mouse dishes, on the other hand, is seldom described in mainstream cookbooks. Given that mice are herbivores, as are most of our other animal food sources (except for fish), one would expect that their meat would have a culturally acceptable flavor. The main disadvantage of the mouse [46] as a human food item is the minimal amount of meat available on each mouse carcass, and the small bones that would either have to be ingested or avoided. Another consideration is that some people would undoubtedly be put off by the appearance of the tail (which, of course, could be removed unless the mouse is to be deep-fried, in which case the tail would be used as a "handle"). Attention has recently been brought to the mouse as food by a recent popular adventure movie (Living with Wolves, 2005) in which the main character took a lesson from his savvy canine friends the wolves, and subsisted on mice during his sojourn in the Arctic winter. There are many subspecies of *Mus musculus*, with one or more in nearly every climactic zone, so perhaps this is a novel food source that deserves exploitation.

CRABS

Many species of crabs in the family Portunidae are edible, but perhaps the best known is the blue crab,[47] *Callinectes sapidus*. It prefers life in the brackish bays of America's east and south coasts, but has been

DEEP-FRIED CHICKEN LIVERS WITH CRAB

Press a chicken liver on a board with the palm of the hand and carefully split it with a knife into 2 thin slices. Repeat for as many livers as desired. Cut pieces of fatty pig mesentery or omentum into pieces 3 inches by 6 inches. Put a drained slice of liver on a rectangle of mesentery, then several pieces of crab meat, a piece of crab roe, and top with another slice of liver. Roll up the mesentery into a small package by first folding in the sides. Deep-fry these packages for 10 minutes. [52]

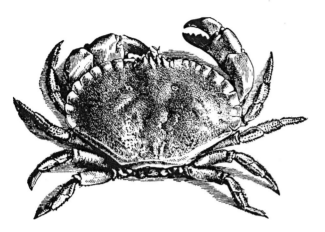

reported as far north as Nova Scotia and as far south as Uruguay. The blue crab is also found on the east coast of South America and has been seen in the coastal waters of France, Holland, and Denmark.[48]

Callinectes sapidus means "beautiful, savory swimmer," and crab lovers would certainly agree with that appellation. The blue crab is one of the more abundant estuarine macroinvertebrates; it is an estuarine-dependent species whose life history involves a complex cycle of planktonic, nektonic, and benthic stages that occur throughout the estuarine-nearshore marine environment in a variety of habitats. The blue crab plays a crucial role in the estuarine food web, providing prey for many species and in turn is a voracious predator on other species.[49] Crabs function much of the time as scavengers, but will also attack and eat any animal they can overpower.

Crabs are generally portrayed as unpleasant, aggressive, and belligerent animals. In many languages, the word "crab" is used to refer to a person with a nasty or querulous disposition, and the Latin word for crab, *cancer*, describes a deadly disease. Although the blue crab was not described taxonomically until 1896, when Dr. Mary Jane Rathbun observed it in the Chesapeake Bay and named it, crabs have been present on earth for eons, and are mentioned in Greek mythology (e.g., a giant crab bit Hercules on the foot as he was fighting the Hydra).[50] The ecological success of the crab is certainly due, at least in part, to its "crabby" personality.

DEVILLED CRABS

1 cup chopped crab meat	2/3 cup white stock
1/4 cup mushrooms, finely chopped	2 egg yolks
2 tbs. butter	2 tbs. sherry wine
2 tbs. flour	1 tsp. finely chopped parsley
	Salt and pepper

Make a sauce of butter, flour, and stock; add egg yolks, seasonings (except parsley), crab meat, and mushrooms. Cook three minutes, add parsley, and cool mixture. Wash and trim crab shells, fill rounding with mixture, sprinkle with stale bread crumbs mixed with a small quantity of melted butter. Crease on top with a case knife, having three lines parallel with each other across shell and three short lines branching from outside parallel lines.[53]

FRICASSEE OF CRABS

Take six nice fat crabs, wash them, and while alive chop off the claws; then clean the rest of the crabs carefully and lay them in a dish. Chop up two onions fine, fry them in a tablespoonful of butter, or butter and lard mixed; when brown and soft stir in a large spoonful of flour, which must also brown nicely; throw in some chopped parsley and a little green onion, and when they are cooked pour on a quart of boiling water—this is the gravy. Now put in the crabs without parboiling. Let them simmer in the gravy for half an hour, and serve with boiled rice. Parboiling crabs destroys their flavor; they should be alive to the last moment.[54]

The crab, like most invertebrates, must shed its rigid shell as it grows, to accommodate its new body size. During its two to three year lifespan, a crab may molt as many as twenty times, each time increasing its size by one quarter to one third. Crabs can also replace lost claws or legs within two molts. In the short period during which the new shell has not yet hardened, the crab is referred to as a "soft-shell," and can be fried and eaten, shell and all. "Hard-shell" crabs are usually eaten after steaming, and the meat is picked from the shell. In either case, it is important to bring the internal temperature of the crab high enough to be sure that a bacterium (*Vibrio parahemolyticus*) commonly present on the outer shell of the crab is killed.[51] Care (and probably gloves!) should be used in handling live crabs, as an injury that breaks the skin can result in blood poisoning from the same bacterium. (In addition to *Vibrio parahemolyticus*, many other species of bacteria and parasites may be present on crabs.)

Crabs can be caught on baited lines, with nets, or, as they are commercially, in baited traps. Only live crabs should be used for human consumption, and they should be eaten immediately following cooking. If they are not to be eaten immediately, the crabs should be cleaned promptly and the meat refrigerated.

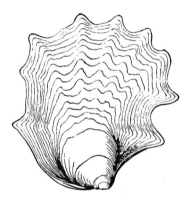

OYSTERS

Oysters [55] of the family Ostreidae, primarily the European oyster, *Ostrea edulis*, and the North American oyster, *Crassostrea virginica*, are bivalve mollusks highly prized in many cultures for their succulent flesh, and have been used as human food for thousands of years. Oysters were so prized by the Romans that they brought them from England, packing them in snow-covered barrels; it is said that when they got back to Rome, they placed them in saltwater pools and fattened them up by feeding them wine and pastries! No Roman orgy was complete without oysters. The Roman Emperor Vitellius was said to have eaten a thousand oysters at a single sitting.

Oysters have exceptional nutritional value; they are high in protein, low in fat, and contain Vitamins A, B, C, D, and E, and high levels of minerals such as calcium, iodine, iron, potassium, copper, and zinc, which are absorbed from the water the oysters filter through their bodies, and which are subsequently incorporated into their flesh. Native Americans on both coasts of North America considered oysters a staple foodstuff, and taught the "new" Americans to appreciate them. Many cultures consider oysters an aphrodisiac; recent scientific evidence suggests that this belief may have merit, possibly due to their high zinc content, which is believed to enhance male fertility.

Oysters are harvested from the wild (where they can be found adhering to rocks, pilings [56], or other fixed objects in relatively shallow salt or brackish water along seacoasts), or, more often, from cultivated and tested populations raised in controlled breeding beds. The growth rate of oysters depends on water temperature and salinity, and if raised under optimal conditions, they are at their gustatory prime at the age of three to four years. However, if spared from harvesting, predation (e.g., by starfish, sea urchins, and octopus) and invasion by parasites (e.g., the oyster drill snail), they may live as long as fifty years.

The size, color, shape, texture, flavor, and nutritional value of the meat of a given oyster depend partly on its species, but largely on its environment and the composition of the water that it filters as it feeds. The shells of wild oysters tend to be rough and irregular, while cultivated oysters have a more uniform shape, and produce more standard meat. The shell shape also depends on the amount of crowding in the oyster bed, and on the species; for instance, *Ostrea* shells are nearly round in shape, while *Crassostrea* are longer than wide, and asymmetrical. Oysters from different geographical regions have distinct, and quite different, flavors. For example, if oysters are raised in water that includes the chlorophyll-containing marine microalga *Navicula ostrearia*, the oysters take on a green tinge, much valued by oyster connoisseurs. In addition to the Atlantic and European oysters, there are the Pacific oyster (*Crassostrea gigas*), the Olympia oyster (*Ostrea lurida*), the Portuguese oyster (*Crassostrea angulata*), and the Japanese oyster (*Crassostrea sikamea*). *Saccostrea glomerata* are harvested in Australia and New Zealand. (Although there are many oyster species, possibly as many as one hundred, only a small percentage have commercial value.)[57]

While abstaining from eating oysters in months whose names do not contain an "r" is an old adage, it is still good advice: Those are the months during which oysters spawn and devote their metabolic energy to reproducing. Warm weather also encourages the growth of bacteria, not a good thing if one prefers to ingest one's oysters raw. As with crabs, only live oysters are safe to eat.

spindled oysters

2 dozen large oysters   6 slices of thin toast

2 ounces bacon   6 steel skewers

Drain, clean, and dry on a soft towel the oysters; cut the bacon in very thin slices. Fill the skewers with bacon and oysters alternately, running the skewer cross-grain through the muscle of the oyster and stringing bits of bacon by one corner so that each slice may overlay an oyster. Do not crowd. Place the skewers across the baking pan and cook over gas or in a quick oven for five minutes. Do not take the oysters from the spindle but lay each one on a slice of toast, pouring over them the drip from the pan.[58]

oyster fritters

Have ready some of the finest and largest oysters; drain them from the liquor and wipe them dry. Beat six eggs very light, and stir into them gradually six tbs. of fine sifted flour. Add by degrees a pint and a half of rich milk and some grated nutmeg, and beat it to a smooth batter. Make your frying pan very hot, and put into it a piece of butter or lard. When it has melted and begins to froth, put in a small ladleful of the batter, drop an oyster in the middle of it, and fry it to a light brown. (If you find your batter too thin, so that it spreads too much in the frying-pan, add a little more flour beaten well into it, or if it is too thick, thin it with some additional milk.) Send them to table hot.[59]

pickled oysters

Take a hundred and fifty fine large oysters, and pick off carefully the bits of shell that may be sticking to them. Lay the oysters in a deep dish, and then strain the liquor over them. Put them into an iron skillet that is lined with porcelain, and add salt to your taste. Without salt they will not be firm enough. Set the skillet on hot coals, and allow the oysters to simmer till they are heated all through, but not till they boil. Then take out the oysters and put them into a stone jar, leaving the liquor in the skillet. Add to it a pint of clear cider vinegar, a large tsp. of blades of mace, three dozen whole cloves, and three dozen whole pepper corns. Let it come to a boil, and when the oysters are quite cold in the jar, pour the liquor on them. They are fit for use immediately, but are better the next day. In cold weather they will keep a week. If you intend sending them a considerable distance you must allow the oysters to boil, and double the proportions of the pickle and spice.[60]

We must regretfully remind optimistic readers that commercially valuable pearls are not generated by members of the edible oyster family; they occur (naturally or with mechanical assistance from humans, to produce what are known as "cultured pearls") only in "pearl oysters" of the family Pteriidae.

Finally, for all of our vegetarian (or squeamish) readers, here is a recipe that utilizes "mock oysters:"

MOCK oysters

4 salsify roots, well-scrubbed

1 egg

1 cup fine breadcrumbs

1/2 tsp. salt

oil for frying

Drop salsify in boiling water and cook until barely tender, about half an hour. Drain, refresh under cold water, and skin. Slice salsify roots diagonally into rounds about 3/4 inch thick. Beat egg in a bowl with 2 tbs. water until frothy. Dip salsify pieces into egg and then into breadcrumbs seasoned with 1/2 tsp. salt, then into the egg and breadcrumbs again. Allow to stand for half an hour and then fry in one inch of hot oil until golden on both sides. Serve with tartar sauce, and garnish with lemon wedges.[61]

CUCUMBERS

The cucumber (*Cucumis sativus*) [62] originated in India between the Bay of Bengal and the Himalayas. The cucumber has been in cultivation for some three thousand years, and is one of the oldest crop vegetables; it is listed and illustrated in *De virtutibus bestiarum in arte medicinae (Apuleius, Dioscorides)*, in Oxford's Bodleian Library. They were grown in North Africa, Italy, Greece, Asia Minor, and other areas at the beginning of the Christian era. In England, the crop was first introduced in the fourteenth century, but not cultivated until two hundred fifty years later, in the seventeenth century. [63]

The cucumber is a warm-season vegetable and a favorite of the British for use in the traditional sandwiches served at tea. In Britian, cucumbers are grown in glass-covered frames that retain heat and compensate for

"after waiting till she fancied she heard the Rabbit just under the window, she suddenly spread out her hand, and made a snatch in the air. She did not get hold of anything, but she heard a little shriek and a fall, and a crash of broken glass, from which she concluded that it was just possible it had fallen into a cucumber-frame, or something of the sort."

"Mmmm," Alice thought, "a nice, fresh cucumber salad would taste wonderful after all this exertion in the heat!" Since the frame had probably been broken beyond repair by the rabbit's fall, and would no longer protect the vegetables, she thought she might as well make good use of the cucumbers right away, while they were nice and fresh.

> ## CHAPTER 4, in which Alice marinates cucumbers, constructs iguana tamales, and learns of the benefits of lizard saliva.

the relatively cool daily temperatures and protect the cucumber plants from fungus problems, which they tend to contract if they remain damp for extended periods of cool weather. It is a certainty that the White Rabbit, a confirmed vegetarian, was quite distraught at the careless destruction of this important garden structure.

CUCUMBER SALAD

Wash and dry two large cucumbers. Trim and discard a thin slice from both ends. With a dinner fork, score the cucumbers along their length, repeating this until they are scored all around their circumference. Slice them thinly and place in a bowl. Also slice one small yellow onion, or four green onions (both the green and white portions), and add them to the bowl. Sprinkle with 2 tbs. chopped parsley, 1 tbs. of sugar, 1/2 tsp. of black pepper, and about 1/3 cup tarragon, malt, or white vinegar. Mix well and refrigerate for an hour or two before serving. [64]

"She drew her foot as far down the chimney as she could, and waited till she heard a little animal (she couldn't guess of what sort it was) scratching and scrambling about in the chimney close above her: then, saying to herself 'This is Bill,' she gave one sharp kick, and waited to see what would happen next... Last came a little feeble, squeaking voice, ('That's Bill,' thought Alice,) 'Well, I hardly know...all I know is, something comes at me like a Jack-in-the-box, and up I goes like a sky-rocket!'"

Alice did feel a little bit sorry about the lizard's mishap, as she was responsible for it. However, her remorse paled in comparison to her desire to have something a little more substantial to go with the cucumber salad she had just made and consumed. She had heard of an exotic dish eaten in Mexico, called tamales, and that when the Mexicans did not have pork or chicken available, they often used large lizards, called iguanas, for the filling. Alice had seen pictures of iguanas in her zoology book. She took a good look at Bill, and observed that he was not so *very* different from an iguana...

LIZARDS

Based solely on Tenniel's rendition, Bill the Lizard may have been a member of the reptilian family *Iguanidae*, a diverse group of relatively mild-mannered lizards. While the smaller members of this family would not provide much meat, Bill's larger Central and South American cousins, the iguanas (e.g., *Iguana iguana*), were traditionally used as a convenient source of animal protein in an environment in which more conventional animal protein sources were scarce. Recently, the increasing population of Central Americans living in or near at least one American city (Washington, D.C.) has provided a lively market for imported iguana meat. The frozen, farm-raised meat, known to El Salvadorans as *garrobo*, can sell for as much as $12.50/lb.[65] In addition to being a protein source, iguana meat is imbued by some with special powers, such as the ability to act as an aphrodisiac, or to cleanse the blood of the mammalian eater. Iguana meat is considered by some to be a "natural energy source" because of the reptile's ability to grow new cells to regenerate its tail. Iguana soup is also purported to cure illnesses, similar to the putative curative attributes of chicken soup. Enjoy your tamales!

34

IGuana Tamales

FILLING:

5 pounds iguana chunks (2-3 iguanas, skinned, cleaned, and trimmed of heads and legs)

1/2 cup diced red pepper   1 cup cubanelle (or similar) peppers, diced

1 habanero pepper, seeds and veins removed, and diced   1 cup diced onion

6 cloves of garlic, crushed   1 tbs. salt   water to cover

Combine all ingredients with water and cook until meat is done. Strain meat and set aside. Reserve liquid for later use.

CORN MEAL MIXTURE:

7 1/2 pounds plain cornmeal   1/4 cup salt   2 1/2 cups fresh ground onion

1/2 cup fresh ground garlic   3 tbs. chile powder   2 tbs. cumin powder

2 tbs. dried oregano

Combine all ingredients and mix well. Add 1 gallon of reserved liquid from meat mixture. Mix well. Let meat and corn meal mixtures cool overnight in refrigerator.

Bring 1 gallon of water to the boil. Meanwhile, spread meal mixture in tamale wrapper. Corn shucks, tamale papers, or banana leaves may be used. Add meat mixture to center. Roll tamales. Tie tamales up with cotton string if necessary. Gently place tamales in the boiling water, and cook for 3 hours. Remove from heat and set aside for 30 minutes. Add more water to cover. Cook for 1 additional hour. (Note: If iguana meat is not available, any other meat can be substituted.)[66]

Some readers may be interested in a curious scientific finding regarding the beneficial properties of lizard saliva. In the search for diabetes treatments, it has been found that the poisonous saliva of the Gila Monster *(Heloderma suspectum)* [67] contains a secretagogue for insulin.

This peptide (exendin-4) is more potent and has a longer half-life in humans and in rodents than other insulinotropic peptides previously examined (gastric inhibitory polypeptide and glucagon-like peptide-1).[68] The implication of this work is that an antidiabetic treatment based on the properties of exendin-4 may eventually become available.

CHAPTER 5, in which Alice learns about noise-making caterpillars, utilizes mushroom flaps, and prepares pigeon water.

CATERPILLARS

Entomophagy dates back to the beginning of human history, and nearly fifteen hundred species of insects have been documented as edible.[69] Insects consumed by humans include crickets, grasshoppers, cicadas, dragonflies, termites, ants (and their larvae and pupae), beetle larvae, wasp pupae (and pre-pupae), and caterpillars (and occasionally pupae) of numerous species of Lepidoptera.

Caterpillars, in particular, are held in high esteem as menu items in many areas of the world. Caterpillars are high in protein; in one study, the average crude protein content (dry weight) for twenty-two species was 64.5%. Compare this to 32% for dried fish, and 22% for dried peas. Caterpillars are

"...the Caterpillar took the hookah out of its mouth and yawned once or twice, and shook itself. Then it got down off the mushroom, and crawled away in the grass, merely remarking as it went, 'One side will make you grow taller, and the other side will make you grow shorter.'

'One side of WHAT? The other side of WHAT?' thought Alice to herself. 'Of the mushroom,' said the Caterpillar, just as if she had asked it aloud; and in another moment it was out of sight."

Alice experimented with pieces from different sides of the mushroom, and finally, with relief, regained her original size. All this effort had exhausted her, and as she could only eat small pieces of the mushroom (because small amounts had great effects on her size), she was very hungry. Although she knew little about such things, she thought that perhaps if the mushroom were cooked, its size-altering capacity would be inactivated. "Hmm," she thought, "meat goes very well with mushrooms." She found a nice long branch nearby that would serve as a skewer, and hunkered down to wait until the caterpillar should reappear.

also rich in fat, and contain essential vitamins (B1, B2, and niacin) and minerals (iron, copper, and zinc); they are so nutritious that they have been described as "Nature's vitamin pills!"[70] Caterpillars are a dietary staple for African, Australian, Middle Eastern, Asian and native South and North American cultures, whose diet is primarily based on grains and would otherwise be deficient in protein and fat. For example, in Zambia, at the beginning of the rainy season, millet starts to become scarce, and mushrooms and caterpillars are the main source of additional "relishes" to meals. In at least one region of the Congo, caterpillars make up 40% of the animal protein consumed, and around forty species are known to be eaten. About a dozen of these are species of Saturniidae (Emperor Moths, or Giant Silk Moths; e.g., *Imbrasia ertli*, *Cirina forda*, and *Bunaeopsis aurantiaca*), but *Anaphe sp.* (Notodontidae), the Sphingidae (Sphinx Moths), and the larva of the *Orycites* beetle (also known as the palm worm) are also important. A table of edible Saturniidae species is provided here.

EDIBLE SATURNIIDAE [71]

Genus and species	Stage(s) at which eaten
Bunaea alcinoe	larva, pupa
Bunaeopsis sp.	larva, pupa
Cinabra hyperbius	larva
Cirina forda	larva, pupa
Gonimbrasia belina	larva, pupa
Gynanisa maia	larva, pupa
Holocerina agomensis	larva
Imbrasia epimethea	larva, pupa
Lobobunaea christyi	larva
Lobobunaea saturnus	larva
Micragone ansorgei	larva

Harvesting caterpillars is fairly simple: Forest-dwelling caterpillar species descend to the base of the food tree for their final molt (which is followed by pupation underground), and are collected there. Aggregations of caterpillars are often identified by the presence of their droppings under trees, and the populations are observed so that they can be harvested at the optimum time. Caterpillars [72] may be prepared and eaten immediately, or dried for future use.

Preparation of caterpillars for cooking may include the removal of spines and/or long hairs by singeing them off over a fire, and, for those species that feed on toxic plants, removal of the gut contents. This is accomplished either by slitting the caterpillars open or by using a pointed stick to turn them inside out. Local preferences vary from here on: The caterpillars may be boiled; roasted (when used as a snack); stewed with peanut butter, peanut sauce, or vegetables (often the preference for preserved caterpillars); mixed with cassava leaves; cooked with pumpkin and sesame seeds; served with porridge as the meat course; or simply fried with salt and a few hot peppers. African silk moth larvae contain a good amount of fat and so can be fried without additional oil; see also specific preparation methods within recipes.[73]

Local cultures prefer different caterpillar species, and have clear ideas about how they should be consumed. Two examples follow.

"A well-liked caterpillar known as *cimbua* [taxonomic name unknown] is without question the caterpillar most often marketed in the Nkoya and Mashasha territories of Zambia. Cimbua larvae taken from the cocoons are considered to be the best of all caterpillars. Their fatness, the nice taste and the softness of their skin are praised. The aroma is compared with that of honey or nectar. The taste is compared with that of fried winged termites. The preferred method of preparation is to roast the larvae in the cocoons. The cocoons burning over the embers give the larvae a 'very nice smoked taste,' which is made more distinct with addition of a little salt." Until used, "the larvae are stored in the cocoons where they remain alive and fat for at least two months."[74]

"The caterpillar of *Gynanisa maia* is considered delicious. It is praised for its enormous size, for its thick layer of fat, and for the nice taste. The fully grown larvae have one important defect, however, from a culinary standpoint. The skin is very thick and leathery and some people complain that they have to chew it for an unreasonable length of time; others like the tough skin, saying it is 'juicy and nice,' and one can chew it a long time before the taste is gone. Most maintain, however, that it is best either when it is moulting or not longer than about fifty to seventy millimeters in length."[75]

This anecdote sums up the extent to which caterpillars are appreciated as a food item: "The larva of *Nephele comma* (of the family Sphingidae, and known locally as *cikilakila*) is highly appreciated as food. It is said that 'when one has eaten one cikilakila, it is hardly possible to check oneself, before all the caterpillars in the pot are finished.'"[76]

The practice of entomophagy is not generally accepted in Western cultures, and even if it were, the caterpillar, with its many "feet," its "hair," and often, toxic (or at least, urticant) spines or extensible appendages, would probably not be the food item of choice. (This is evident in the countries of origin of the recipes offered here.) Sadly, European anti-entomophagy influences in Africa are diminishing the incidence of this nutritious practice.

39

ROASTED PALM-WORMS WITH ORANGE JUICE (FRENCH WEST INDIES)

Skewer the palm worms and roast over charcoal. Roll in a mixture of fine bread crumbs, salt, pepper, and nutmeg and sprinkle with orange juice. Return to the fire to brown.[79]

FRIED PALMWORMS (VIETNAM)

Dip the grubs in nuoc-mam sauce and fry in lard. Wrap in pastry and refry. Or simply roll in flour and fry in butter.[80]

ROASTED BEETLE GRUBS (SAMOA)

Feed the larvae on coconut shavings for a day. Then wrap them in a banana or other suitable leaf and roast over charcoal.[81]

SILKWORM OMELET (CHINA)

After reeling the silk from the cocoon, bake and salt silkworm pupae. Then soften them in water. Mix with beaten chicken eggs and fry in oil as a flat omelet.[82]

Methods for preparing caterpillars for consumption:[77]

Before cooking or drying, the large varieties of caterpillars are "gutted" by opening the mouthpart with a bit of stick and squeezing the caterpillar like a concertina between finger and thumb. If cooked fresh, the caterpillars are then washed, placed in a pot with cold water and boiled for one and a half hours. Salt is added. Caterpillars are dried after gutting by roasting over a fire for three to four hours and then spreading out on a mat in the sun for three to four days. They are stored in sacks or clay pots. Before cooking they are washed in hot water and then placed in a pot with cold water and boiled for thirty minutes. Alternatively, they may be roasted on the fire for a few minutes and eaten dry.

Smooth caterpillars are the best, and they should be cooked or frozen while alive; once insects die, they can become unpalatable. Place them in a kitchen colander, rinse in cool water, drain, pat dry with a paper towel and use immediately or freeze in a plastic bag for later use. You may want to remove the legs and head; if you prefer to remove parts, the procedure works best when the insect is frozen or already dry roasted.

In general, it is best to crush or use a blender on your insects and cook in a stew to disguise their appearance. If at any time you find you cannot eat your gathered insects, do not despair. Boil them in a pot of water. The fat will rise to the top. Scoop it up and drink.

Dry insects placed on a paper towel can be baked on a cookie sheet at 150 to 200°F for at least one hour until dried. An alternative is to freeze the insects in a plastic bag overnight, then blanch them to remove any debris or contaminants. Next, take off the heads and legs and bake them for about two hours until dry. You will now have an insect that can be used in most recipes. In the outdoors, they can be killed and then placed on a hot rock to be solar dried.[78]

It is interesting to note, in light of the Wonderland caterpillar's conversation with Alice, that the caterpillar of at least one lepidopteran species, *Drepana arcuata*, can generate sounds. It drums its mandibles and scrapes specialized anal "oars" against a leaf, presumably to defend its nest and intimidate intruders.[85]

Fried Silkworm Pupae and Onions (China)

Soak baked or salted pupae in water. Drain and stir-fry in a little oil to which sliced onions and a little soy sauce have been added.[83]

If the reader encounters difficulty in obtaining palmworms, beetle grubs, or silkworms, here is a recipe that calls for a native American caterpillar, one that most gardeners will be thrilled to see fried:

Fried Green Tomato Hornworms (USA)

3 tbs. olive oil
16 tomato hornworms
4 medium green tomatoes, sliced 1/4 inch thick
salt and pepper to taste
white cornmeal

In a large skillet, heat the oil. Lightly fry the hornworms on high heat, about 4 minutes, taking care not to rupture the cuticles of each insect. Remove with a slotted spoon and set aside. Season tomato rounds with salt and pepper, and coat with cornmeal on both sides. Fry tomatoes until lightly browned on both sides. Remove the tomatoes to plates and top each slice with 2 fried tomato hornworms. Garnish the paired hornworms with a single basil leaf.[84]

MUSHROOMS

Mushrooms are the spore-bearing (reproductive) structures of the fungi, which constitute the largest plant group on earth. They are found in virtually every climate and habitat. Because fungi contain no chlorophyll (the source of energy, through photosynthesis, for many plants), they must acquire energy by other mechanicsms. Some are saprophytes and obtain energy by enzymatic decompostion of dead plant and animal material; others are parasites on living plants or animals. Some one hundred thousand species of fungi have been described, and scientists estimate that as many as two hundred thousand more await discovery."[86] While many fungi cause diseases in animals and humans, and damage crops and other plants, many others, such as yeast and penicillin, are beneficial to humans. Virtually every culture on earth makes use of mushrooms [87], for food, medicine, fabric dyes, or ritualistic purposes.

Many species of mushrooms are cultivated and commercially available. Certain wild mushrooms are edible, but many are poisonous, so caution should be used in collecting fungi from the wild. Mushrooms come in all shapes, sizes, and colors. Mushroom hunters say that all species of mushrooms are edible, but that some are only edible by a given individual *once*. There is an old adage on this subject: "There are old mushroom hunters and bold mushroom hunters, but there are no old, bold mushroom hunters."[88]

41

When it comes to identifying edible fungi, none of the following statements is true:

- **Poisonous mushrooms tarnish a silver spoon.**
- **If it peels, you can eat it.**
- **All mushrooms growing on wood are edible.**
- **Mushrooms that squirrels or other animals eat are safe for humans.**
- **All mushrooms in meadows and pastures are safe to eat.**
- **All white mushrooms are edible.**
- **Poisonous mushrooms can be detoxified by parboiling, drying, or pickling.**
- **A clove of garlic turns black when cooked with a poisonous mushroom.**[89]

In addition to the edible mushrooms, and the definitely poisonous ones, there are quite a number that are only mildly poisonous, or are hallucinogenic, or both. It is likely that the mushroom on which Carroll's caterpillar was sitting was of this type. The most common hallucinogenic toxins are psilocybin and psilocin, which, chemically, are in the LSD family of hallucinogenic compounds.

The drawing shows "Your brain on mushrooms."[90] The active ingredients in these mushrooms have a strong effect on the central nervous system, producing such effects as visions, smothering sensations, and optical distortions such as those Alice experienced. Some victims have reported experiencing religious or mystical experiences. However, "bad trips" may also occur, and induce anxiety or even paranoia in the victim; these pathological states can be severe enough to require medical treatment. The quantity of the toxin ingested, and the physiological condition, personality, and mood of the subject are all apparently involved in the type and degree of effect. Other toxins in addition to the primary hallucinogenic agent may be present in a particular mushroom, and this may contribute to the psychoactive effects.[91]

While mushrooms have little protein and no fat, they do contain minerals, and their various flavors complement many other foods. They can be used in any variety of culinary ways; a few recipes are printed.

Baked mushrooms

16 to 20 mushroom flaps
butter
salt
pepper to taste

For this mode of cooking, mushroom flaps are better than buttons, and should not be too large. Cut off a portion of the stalk, peel the top, and wipe the mushrooms carefully with a piece of cloth and a little fine salt. Put them into a baking tin, with a very small piece of butter placed on each mushroom; sprinkle over a little pepper, and let them bake for about 20 minutes, or longer should the mushrooms be very large. Have ready a very hot dish, pile the mushrooms high in the center, pour the cooking liquid around, and send them to table quickly, with very hot plates.[92]

Some readers may find it interesting that while Carroll's caterpillar seemed to have a more or less symbiotic relationship with the mushroom (less, when the caterpillar was offering chunks of it to passersby...), paradoxically, in nature, many caterpillars meet their demise as a result of infection by fungi of the parasitic genus *Cordyceps*. Moreover, such infected caterpillars (dead, shriveled, and with a filament of the fungal growth emanating from them that may be longer than the caterpillars themselves) are gathered in China and used as tonics and as food. They are also made into a broth, with both caterpillars and cooking liquid being consumed.[95]

MUSHROOM KETCHUP

8 pounds mushrooms	1/2 pound salt

Choose full-grown mushroom flaps, and take care they are perfectly fresh-gathered when the weather is tolerably dry, for if they are picked during very heavy rain, the ketchup which is made from them is liable to get musty, and will not keep long.

Put a layer of mushrooms in a deep pan, sprinkle salt over them, and then another layer of mushrooms, and so on, alternately. Let them stand for a few hours, then break them up with the hand; put them in a nice cool place for 3 days, occasionally stirring and mashing well to extract from them as much juice as possible. Now measure the quantity of liquor, and to every 2 pints, add:

1/2 ounce cayenne	1/2 ounce allspice
1/2 ounce ground ginger	2 blades pounded mace

Put all into a jar, including the mushrooms, cover it up very tightly, put it in a saucepan of boiling water, set it over the heat, and let it boil for 3 hours. Have ready a nice clean stewpan; turn into it the contents of the jar, and let the whole simmer very gently for half an hour; pour it into a jug, where it should stand in a cool place till the next day; then strain it off into another jug, taking care not to squeeze the mushrooms; be careful also to leave all the sediment behind in the jug. To each pint of ketchup, add a few drops of brandy, then strain again into very dry clean bottles; cork well so as to exclude air perfectly. [93]

MUSHROOM CURRY

1 pound fresh mushrooms	1 large onion, chopped	1 clove garlic, crushed red pepper to taste
2 tbs. oil or margarine	1 onion, thinly sliced in rings	1 tbs. lime or lemon juice
1/2 tsp. turmeric powder	salt to taste	

Remove all the dirt from the mushrooms by washing in water to which 1 tbs. of flour has been added; it will make them beautifully white. (Do not peel them.) Use whole if small, or cut into quarters if large. Combine mushrooms with the chopped onion, garlic, and spices. Heat oil in a frying pan, add mushrooms, spices, and sliced onion. Saute for about 10 minutes, stirring frequently. Add citrus juice and serve with rice, or thicken slightly with flour browned in margarine and serve on slices of dried bread.[94]

"... a large pigeon had flown into her face, and was beating her violently with its wings...

'Well! WHAT are you?' said the Pigeon...

...'I — I'm a little girl,' said Alice, rather doubtfully, as she remembered the number of changes she had gone through that day.

'A likely story indeed!' said the Pigeon in a tone of the deepest contempt. 'I've seen a good many little girls in my time, but never ONE with such a neck as that! No, no! You're a serpent; and there's no use denying it. I suppose you'll be telling me next that you never tasted an egg!'

'I HAVE tasted eggs, certainly,' said Alice, who was a very truthful child; 'but little girls eat eggs quite as much as serpents do, you know...but I'm not looking for eggs, as it happens; and if I was, I shouldn't want YOURS: I don't like them raw.'...

... 'Well, be off, then!' said the Pigeon in a sulky tone, as it settled down again into its nest."

Alice had found the Pigeon extremely annoying, and all the effort of defending herself against the bird had made her quite hungry. Alice had eaten pigeon pie before, and while she thought it must be very difficult to prepare, she was motivated to try to do it. She figured as long as the pigeon was going into the pie, she might as well use the little eggs, too.

PIGEONS

The term "pigeon" most often refers to the varicolored, stout, sleek, and often pestiferous common pigeon, *Columba livia*, and its some two hundred derived domestic varieties; it can refer also to various types of doves. However, the "pigeon" in Carroll's story is most likely the common British wood pigeon, *Columba palumbus*, which is mostly gray in color, with a pinkish breast and a roundish white spot on the neck, edged in purple.

Doves and pigeons have figured prominently in human history, long before one of them appeared in *Alice's Adventures in Wonderland*. They were an object of religious worship from the earliest times, and appear in early Egyptian and Roman writings, as well as in the Bible. They were also the subjects of many legends and fables, and represented the spirit of renewal in the quest for the Holy Grail. The Greeks bred and reared homing pigeons thousands of years ago, and these special pigeons were widely used during wartime for carrying secret military messages. In fact, pigeons remained one of the safest ways to send messages through the end of the Vietnam War, when electronic devices began to make the birds' messenger skills obsolete. Pigeons are also bred and trained to race (a competitive sport enjoyed by many), and have proven to be a useful model for many genetic studies. Last (but not least!), pigeons have been a staple of the human diet for centuries; in some American states, e.g., Texas, there is a legal "season" for hunting doves.[96]

A favored way to prepare small birds for the table is in the form of pies. Such pies have traditionally been made and consumed by many cultures in many areas of the world; Britain, Scotland, France, Italy, Corsica, Spain, and Morocco are just a few. The Moroccan version of pigeon pie, "bstila"(or "bastilla,"or "pastilla," or "bestilla"), is a traditional dish eaten with the fingers from a common bowl. This dish was developed in times of poor food supply, but it is nevertheless enjoyed in more abundant times as a great delicacy, and served on special occasions. In addition to the birds, it contained almonds, cinnamon, sugar, and saffron. The British version *(recipe below)* is less exotic.

There is at least one use for pigeons in addition to their use as food:

Beauty-conscious ladies of the court in seventeenth-century Paris recommended washing the face with "pigeon water" twice a day!

PIGEON PIE

1 1/2 pounds rump steak	2 or 3 pigeons	3 slices of ham
pepper and salt to taste	2 ounces butter	4 eggs
1/2 pound puff paste	1/2 pint of medium stock	

Cut the steak into pieces about 3 inches square, and with them line the bottom of a pie dish, seasoning them well with pepper and salt. Clean the pigeons, rub them with pepper and salt inside and out, and put into the body of each rather more than 1/2 ounce of butter; lay them on the steak, with a piece of ham on each pigeon. Add the yolks of 4 eggs, and half fill the dish with the stock; place a border of puff paste round the edge of the dish, put on the cover, and ornament it in any way that may be preferred. Clean three of the feet, and place them in a hole made in the crust at the top; this shows what kind of pie it is. Glaze the crust, that is to say, brush it over with the yolk of an egg, and bake it in a moderate oven for about 1 1/4 hours. When liked, a seasoning of pounded mace may be added.[97]

PIGEON WATER

Take two white pigeons, pull them, and cast away the guts, head, wings, and legs. Then mince them into small pieces, put them into a glass alembic, strewing the bottom with some plantain leaves. Add thereto 3 ounces of oil of almonds, 4 ounces of butter, a pint of goat's milk, the crumb of a white loaf, two drams each of borax and sugar candy, 3 drams each of burnt alum and powdered camphor, and the whites of 24 eggs. Let all these infuse for the space of 12 hours. Then carefully stop [insert a stopper into] the alembic, and distill them.[98]

PIGS

Archeologists believe that pigs appeared on our planet about forty million years ago. Apparently, humans saw their potential early on, since pigs were one of the first animals to be domesticated and trained by humans, around 7000 B.C. Pigs have held an honored place in history from the time of the ancient Egyptians and Chinese to the present. We revere pigs not only as a source of nutrition, but as principal characters in cartoons and movies.

Around 4000 B.C., the Chinese Emperor decreed that his people raise and breed pigs.[99] Although they apparently had no difficulty eating pigs, the Chinese people became so attached to these animals that they did not want to leave them, even in death, and were often buried with them. Around the same era in Egypt, pigs were also prized, and were eaten only once a year.

In 1492, Queen Isabella of Spain insisted that Christopher Columbus take pigs on his voyage across the Atlantic to introduce fresh pork to the New World. George Washington imported certain varieties of pigs from Europe to establish breeding herds on his estate. One of these types was the Hampshire, a breed from the British Isles noted (and often

CHAPTER 6, in which Alice learns about pettitoes, what it means to live high on the hog, and the origin of "Uncle Sam."

criticized) for its large size, but admired for its prolificacy, hardy vigor, foraging ability, and outstanding carcass qualities. It is said that in the development of the famous Smithfield Ham, only Hampshire pigs were used.[100]

"The baby grunted again, and Alice looked very anxiously into its face to see what was the matter with it. There could be no doubt that it had a VERY turn-up nose, much more like a snout than a real nose; also its eyes were getting extremely small for a baby: altogether Alice did not like the look of the thing at all…

Alice was just beginning to think to herself, 'Now, what am I to do with this creature when I get it home?' when it grunted again, so violently, that she looked down into its face in some alarm. This time there could be NO mistake about it: it was neither more nor less than a pig, and she felt that it would be quite absurd for her to carry it further," unless it was into the kitchen, to be turned into something edible. (By this time, the effort of carrying the pig around had made Alice quite peckish.)

"A roast of pork would be quite delicious," she thought, and planned on preparing one, but Alice had been taught not to be wasteful, so she considered how best to use the remaining parts of the animal as well…

PIG'S Trotters

4 pig's trotters or pettitoes
1/2 pound pig's liver
1/2 pound pig's heart
1 thin slice of bacon
1 onion
1 blade of mace
6 peppercorns
3-4 sprigs of thyme
1 pint of gravy
pepper and salt to taste
thickening of butter and flour

Put the liver, heart, and pettitoes into a stewpan with the bacon, mace, peppercorns, thyme, onion, and gravy, and simmer these gently for 1/4 hour; then take out the heart and liver, and mince them very fine. Keep stewing the feet until quite tender, which should be in 20 to 30 minutes, reckoning from the time that they boiled up first; then put back the minced liver and heart, thicken the gravy with a little butter and flour, season with pepper and salt, and simmer over a gentle heat for 5 minutes, occasionally stirring. Dish the mince, split the feet, and arrange them around alternately with sippets of toasted bread, and pour the gravy in the middle.[104]

With much scientific effort, leaner pork gradually evolved, and pork today compares favorably, with regard to fat, calories, and cholesterol, to many other meats and poultry. Many cuts of pork are as lean or leaner than chicken. Any cuts from the loin, such as pork chops and pork roast, are leaner than skinless chicken thigh, according to U.S. Department of Agriculture data.[101]

Pigs have participated, or have been featured, in some important events in history, and are responsible for a number of sayings in common use today. We offer here some pork facts and fiction that readers may find interesting:[102]

During the War of 1812, a New York pork packer named "Uncle" Sam Wilson shipped a boatload of several hundred barrels of pork to U.S. troops. Each barrel was stamped "U.S." on the docks, and it was quickly said that the "U.S." stood for "Uncle Sam," whose large shipment seemed to be enough to feed the entire army. This is one version of how "Uncle Sam" came to represent the U.S. Government.

The city of Cincinnati, Ohio, was nicknamed "Porkopolis" in 1863 because it was a major pork processing center.

Free-roaming hogs were famous for rampaging through the valuable grain fields of colonial New York City farmers. The Manhattan Island residents chose to block the troublesome hogs with a long, permanent wall on the northern edge of what is now Lower Manhattan. A street came to border this wall, named, aptly enough, Wall Street.

The heaviest hog in history was a 1933 Poland China named "Big Bill." The hog weighed 2,552 pounds and measured nine feet long, with a belly that dragged on the ground.

President Truman said that "No man should be allowed to be President who does not understand hogs."

Enlisted men in the U.S. Army received meat from the shoulder and leg cuts of pork,[103] while officers received the top loin cuts. So "living high on the hog" came to mean living well.

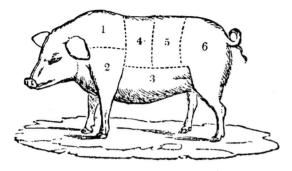

The highest price ever paid for a pig to be used for meat was $56,000, for a crossbreed hog named "Bud," on March 5, 1985. However, the sale of Myrna, a trained French truffle-hunting pig, brought $150,000. (Needless to say, Myrna was not eaten as meat, and, in fact, had life insurance, which was paid out when she died of natural causes at the age of fifteen years.)

For years, the British royal family kept a large herd of pigs at Windsor Castle.

It was once the practice at fairs to grease a pig and let it loose among a number of blindfolded contestants. The person who successfully caught the greased pig could keep it, hence the saying "bring home the bacon."

The expression "to go whole hog" originated in the eighteenth century; the English shilling was at one time called a "hog." To be willing to spend a whole shilling on something like the entertainment of a friend was to "go the hog." As long as we are considering the "whole hog," there are many recipes that utilize parts of the pig other than the more popular roasts and hams; here are a few.

PIG'S FACE AND CABBAGE (IRELAND)

Cut the meat from one side of a pig's head in one piece. Soak it in cold water overnight and boil it (15 minutes per pound) with a head of cabbage. Score the skin and bake the face, skin-side up, in a 350°F oven until the cracklings are crisp and well-browned. Drain and chop the cabbage and arrange it on a platter around the face. Serve with a sauce made with the pan drippings.[105]

ROASTED HOG'S MAW (PENNSYLVANIA DUTCH)

Make a 3-inch incision in the stomach where the esophagus joins, turn it inside out, and clean it. Stuff the stomach loosely with a mixture of seasoned sausage meat, bread, diced potatoes, chopped parsley, salt, and pepper. Sew it shut. Roast it for 2 to 3 hours.[106]

PIG UTERUS SAUSAGE (ANCIENT ROME)

Stuff the uterus of a pig with a mixture of cumin, pepper, leeks, garum, pounded pork meat, and pine nuts. Cook the "sausage" in water and oil with some garum, dill, and leeks added.[107]

RECIPE FOR PIGTAILS (FRANCE)

Scald pigtails and immerse them in brine for 2 to 3 days. Put them into a kettle with clove-stuck onions, sliced leeks and carrots, peppercorns, a bouquet garni, and water to cover. Simmer for 2 hours. Cut the tails into pieces and serve them on mashed potatoes with chopped parsley. Reduce some of the stock for a sauce.[108]

DOTTLE GRUEL

"Dottle," Alice knew, was a Scotch word for a thick brown plug of tobacco left unsmoked in a pipe. Robert Gilbert included a recipe for "Dottle Gruel" in his *Moose Mousse and Other Exotic Recipes*[109] in a fruitless attempt to rescue dottle from the ignominy into which it has deservedly fallen since the eighteenth century. (Dottle Gruel was disdained even by Oliver Twist.) Here, nonetheless, is Gilbert's recipe, in case you are feeling more adventuresome than Alice:

> ### DOTTLE GRUEL
> Soak 4 cups of dottle in a bit of water overnight and simmer in an iron pot for 20 minutes just prior to serving. Dottle is generally unavailable in better shops, so you had better plan ahead and conserve your own. Serve with brown sugar and cream.

CHAPTER 7, in which Alice is introduced to dottle gruel and jugged hare, and learns more than she wanted to know about treacle wells and dormouse husbandry.

"There was a table set out under a tree in front of the house, and the March Hare and the Hatter were having tea at it: a Dormouse was sitting between them, and the other two were resting their elbows on it, and talking over its head ..." "At least," Alice thought, "they won't be having Dottle Gruel at this time of day!"

"The table was a large one, but the three were all crowded together at one corner of it: 'No room! No room!' they cried out when they saw Alice coming. 'There's PLENTY of room!' said Alice indignantly, and she sat down in a large arm-chair at one end of the table…

'If you knew Time as well as I do,' said the Hatter, 'you wouldn't talk about wasting IT. It's HIM.' 'Now, if you only kept on good terms with him, he'd do almost anything you liked with the clock. For instance, suppose it were nine o'clock in the morning, just time to begin lessons: you'd only have to whisper a hint to Time, and round goes the clock in a twinkling! Half-past one, time for dinner!' ('I only wish it was,' the March Hare said to itself in a whisper.) 'That would be grand, certainly,' said Alice thoughtfully…" She couldn't have agreed more with the Hare. She was, of course, quite hungry, as there was not much available on the tea-table, and listening to the Hatter's arguments had quite tired her out. As the March Hare apparently had little awareness of reality, it should be a simple matter to turn it into a tasty dish of jugged hare, which would be very welcome right about now…

HARES

"Jugged" hare is a traditional, even classic, English dish that utilizes the meat, organs, and blood of the hare, and so called because it was cooked in a tall "jug" or crock set into a pan of water. E. Cobham Brewer defines it thus: "The hare being cut up is put into a jug or pipkin, and the pipkin is set in a pan of water. This bain marie prevents the contents of the pipkin from being burnt." [110] The blood and liver may be added to the dish before cooking, or kept separate and used in a sauce (blood mixed with cream and the pulverized hare liver) and poured over the dish when it is done.

JUGGED HARE

1 hare	1 1/2 pounds shin beef
1/2 pound butter	1 onion
1 lemon	6 cloves
pepper	cayenne
salt to taste	1/2 pint of port
flour	

Skin, paunch, and wash the hare, cut it into pieces, dredge them with flour, and fry in butter. Have ready 1 1/2 pints of gravy, made from the above proportion of beef and thickened with a little flour. Put this into a jar; add the pieces of fried hare, an onion stuck with the cloves, a lemon peeled and cut in half, and a good seasoning of pepper, cayenne, and salt; cover the jar down tightly, put it up to the neck into a stewpan of boiling water, and let it stew until the hare is quite tender, taking care to keep the water boiling. When nearly done, pour in the port, and add a few balls of forcemeat; these must be fried or baked in the oven for a few minutes before they are put into the gravy. Serve with red currant jelly. [111]

TREACLE

Treacle is a generic word used in Great
Britain for any syrup made in the process
of refining sugar cane, and it can range
from very light to very dark. In practice,
the lighter syrup, which is produced
when the sugar cane juice is first boiled,
is called light treacle [112] or golden syrup.

The second boiling produces a much darker syrup, which
British cooks call treacle and which Americans call molasses
(or dark molasses). The third boiling produces what is known,
on both sides of the Atlantic, as blackstrap molasses; it is very
dark and somewhat bitter. Although it is used for some cooking
purposes, it is more often utilized in cattle feed. [113]

A large body of folklore has built up about treacle "mining,"
probably as a result of an event that occurred in 1853, the
review by Queen Victoria of eight thousand troops (and fifteen
hundred horses) of the British Army at Staple Hill, Chobham.
To support so many soldiers, an entire community was set
up, with a slaughterhouse, a hospital, stores, canteens, and a
tavern. The review by the Queen was a great success. When the
site was dismantled, the soldiers may have buried some barrels
that had contained treacle (but were probably filled with water
rather than valuable treacle, which could easily have been sold
on the black market) to reduce the bulk of materials that had
to be removed. Gullible villagers who sought to unearth the
buried treacle barrels were called "treacle miners." The lore
of treacle mining lives on, and has been extended (fancifully)
back into history to the Romans, when they occupied
England. [114]

The idea of the "treacle well" mentioned by Carroll in this
chapter of *Alice's Adventures in Wonderland* (written just a few
years after the 1853 event) may have originated from the legend
of the buried treacle barrels. However, it is just as likely that
it came from a much older tradition: Ancient cultures revered
bodies of water to the degree that many of them were held as
holy. Lakes, rivers, springs, and wells were often named for
spirits, deities, or saints, and imbued with miraculous healing
powers. Many such "healing wells" survive in England, with as
many as nineteen in and around Oxford alone. [115] That these

*" 'Once upon a time there were
three little sisters,' the Dormouse
began in a great hurry; 'and
their names were Elsie, Lacie,
and Tillie; and they lived at the
bottom of a well—'*

*'What did they live on?' said
Alice, who always took a great
interest in questions of eating
and drinking.*

*'They lived on treacle,' said
the Dormouse, after thinking a
minute or two..."*

Alice loved treacle herself,
but had never heard of living
solely on that! She did,
however, know of a couple of
desserts made with treacle,
and set off for the kitchen
to prepare something that
would go down nicely after the
jugged hare dish.

wells are known as "treacle wells" is confusing, because, as Alice said (correctly, in one sense), "There's no such thing!"

Two facts help clarify this apparent paradox:[116]

    a. The use of the word "treacle" (origin: Greek, *theriake*; Latin, *theriaca*, an antidote to the bite of a wild animal) to mean "healing" or "therapeutic" substantially predates the use of the same word for the sweet, viscous, molasses-like liquid described above.

    b. Healing potions known as *theriaca* (and kept in labeled jars such as those shown here, at left) [117] were compounded by many different physicians independently, each using his own secret formula. The various formulae might include a wide array of ingredients, but routinely required the flesh of a viper. (There was considerable argument among physicians about which vipers were "effective.") These potions were named for the cities in which they were manufactured; thus, there were London Treacle, Flanders Treacle, and so forth. The picture (above, right) shows *theriaca* being prepared in Strasbourg.[118]

Eventually, wells whose water was thought to induce healing or effect miraculous cures came to be known as "treacle wells." Children are still taken to some of these wells, given a glass jar on a string, and encouraged to lower it into the well to draw "treacle." (Kind of a mean trick, the authors think!)

In fact, according to one source, Alice Liddell and her sisters often visited a treacle well at St. Margaret's Church, in Binsey, near Oxford. "The treacle from this well had been noted for centuries as a cure for eye problems. In the eighth century, St. Frideswide, the patron saint of Oxford, appealed for divine intervention to help cure the king's blindness. The treacle well duly appeared, Frideswide cured the king (who had been struck blind because of his lascivious pursuit of the virginal saint), and the well and its treacle were famed throughout, well, Oxford."[119]

Black Treacle Scones

3 2/3 cups all-purpose flour	2 tsp. baking soda	4 1/2 tsp. cream of tartar
1/2 tsp. salt	1 tsp. ground cinnamon	1/4 tsp. ground allspice
1/4 tsp. ground cloves	1/4 tsp. ground nutmeg	1/4 tsp. ground ginger
1/2 cup butter	2 tbs. molasses	1 cup milk

Preheat oven to 425°F. Lightly grease a baking sheet.

In a large bowl, sift together flour, baking soda, cream of tartar, salt, cinnamon, allspice, cloves, nutmeg, and ginger. Cut in butter with fork or pastry blender. Combine milk and molasses in a small bowl; stir into flour mixture until moistened. Turn out dough onto a lightly floured surface and knead briefly. Roll dough out to a half-inch thick round. Cut out circles with a medium biscuit cutter and place pieces on prepared baking sheet so that they are barely touching. Bake in preheated oven for 10 to 12 minutes. Move to a wire rack to cool slightly before serving. For soft scones, cover with a dry cloth for 10 minutes. For crisp scones, do not cover.[120]

Treacle Tart

1 9-inch pie shell, with additional pastry for lattice top	2 cups treacle	1 tsp. lemon juice
1 egg, beaten with 1 tsp. water	1 1/2 cups fresh white breadcrumbs	

Mix the syrup, breadcrumbs, and lemon juice and spread them into the pie shell. Roll out the remaining pastry, cut it into 1/4 inch strips and form a lattice top over the filling. Brush the pastry with the egg and water mixture and bake at 350°F for 10 minutes. Reduce the heat to 300°F and bake for another 20 to 25 minutes or until the filling is lightly set. Serve hot with whipped cream.[121]

Treacle Pudding

6 ounces self-rising flour	3 ounces softened butter or shredded suet
2 ounces granulated sugar	1 egg
6 tbs. milk	2 tbs. treacle

Grease a 2-pint pudding basin if making a steamed pudding, or a deep dish if baking the pudding. Mix together the flour, butter or suet, and sugar. Make a well in the center and add the egg and enough milk to give a soft dropping consistency. Spoon the treacle into the bottom of the prepared dish and then pour in the pudding mixture. If steaming the pudding, cover with pleated greaseproof paper or foil and secure with string. Steam for 1 1/2 to 2 hours. If baking, cook uncovered at 350°F for about 1 hour, until risen. Serve hot with custard.[122]

TREACLE RINGS

Filling:

2 pounds treacle	7 ounces sugar
an equal volume	2 tbs. jam
of water, measured in the treacle tin	14 ounces semolina
zest of a tangerine, an orange, and a lemon	a small amount of candied peel
a pinch of ground cloves	

The filling should be made the day before; it will keep for several days.

To make the filling, place the ingredients, except the semolina, in a saucepan. Bring to the boil and thicken with semolina, adding half at a time. Cook for a few minutes. Meanwhile, make the pastry.

Pastry:

1 3/4 pounds flour	2 egg yolks	1 tbs. butter	water to bind

Sieve the flour, rub in the butter and bind with egg yolks and water. (The pastry will keep for a few days in the refrigerator, wrapped in a plastic bag.)

Divide the pastry into 6 pieces, and roll out one piece at a time. Shape into a rectangle and out of this cut individual rectangles, 4 inches wide and 7 inches long. Take a dessertspoonful of the stuffing and (using semolina on a board) shape it into a sausage shape, as thick as an outsize finger and as long as the pastry rectangle. Put the treacle "sausage" in the center of one of the rectangles and fold the pastry over it. There is no need to damp[en] the edges. Now bring the two edges of pastry together to form a ring. Sprinkle the baking trays with semolina. Put each ring on the baking tray. Now take a sharp knife and slash the pastry with the point of the knife so that the stuffing shows through. Bake in a moderate oven for about 20 minutes, or until pastry is barely colored. The pale pastry makes a striking contrast with the dark pocket of treacle.[123]

DORMICE

The Romans considered dormice a delicacy, so much so that they actually went to the trouble of cultivating them in small earthenware jugs with ventilation holes, called "dolia." These miniature dolia were patterned after the large (five hundred liter capacity) jugs routinely used to store supplies such as grain, oil, and wine; intact examples have been found at Pompeii and other sites. The dormouse dolia were kept in special enclosures, or "gardens," called "gliraria."[124]

If you are interested in pursuing this recipe[125], then you will want to obtain enough dolia (such as the one shown below)[108] to house all the dormice you intend to fatten, and set up a glirarium. [Figure one per person if you are using *Glis glis* (see below); they are about 6 inches long.] The dolia should be furnished with soft nesting material in the bottom, but anything similar will do, as long as it does not allow the dormouse much room to exercise, and keeps the animal in the dark. (This would be an excellent use for all those teapots in your collection that are just sitting on the shelf gathering dust. As Lewis Carroll fans know, dormice love to sleep in them.)

Also have on hand a large supply of fruit, nuts (hazelnuts are preferred), and insects; dormice have prodigious appetites. Plan to take a leave of absence from work, as you will be spending a lot of time feeding the dormice. (Or hire a professional dormouse-sitter or one of the Dormouseketeers from the old "Dickey Dormouse Club.")

"...the last time she saw them, they were trying to put the Dormouse into the teapot." This reminded Alice of something that she had learned in her Latin lessons: that the Romans cultivated dormice in pottery vessels very like teapots, until they became fat enough to eat... This sounded like a good idea to Alice. Although she was quite full, at the moment, of jugged hare and treacle tart, she knew that fattening up the little dormouse might take some time, so she decided to start on that project right away.

Worldwide, the dormouse family Gliridae consists of ten genera and twenty-eight species. In England, there are only two species, one of which is the native *Muscardinus avellanarius*, (the common, or hazel, dormouse). This species is completely protected and may not be collected. The other species, *Glis glis* (the "edible," or "fat," dormouse), was introduced to Britain from mainland Europe in 1902 by Walter (Lord) Rothschild. (The actual country of origin of these imported dormice is uncertain; sources variously state Germany, Switzerland, or Hungary.)

The British legal status of *Glis glis* is a bit confused. Although it is protected by the Berne Convention, trapping permits may be obtained based on damage to commercial crops or timber. To make things even more confusing, a project initiated in recent years by English Nature in Cornwall to provide nest boxes to *encourage* dormice to breed has begun to pay off: The first pair of dormice used one of the nest boxes, built a nest of honeysuckle bark inside, and produced a litter of four young. The paradox is that although the dormouse is protected (and now, apparently, encouraged!), it is an introduced species and trapped animals may not be released back into the wild. This implies that all trapped animals must be killed. The dilemma seems to have an obvious solution: Eat them!

So, in August (or early September at the latest; dormice hibernate for about half the year), obtain a permit to collect *Glis glis*. This should not be difficult to accomplish, as orchardists and owners of woodlands do not appreciate their predations. As the dormice have been feasting in orchards and woodlands for several months, they should be in excellent physical condition.

At night, armed with a flashlight, a net, and a pillowcase, enter the orchard or woodland specified on your permit. Find some dormice. It is easy to distinguish *Glis glis* from *Muscardinus avellanarius*: the former is about eight inches long, and looks much like a squirrel, with a large, fluffy tail; the latter is tiny, only half the size. Catch them in the net, and then gently dump them into the pillowcase. Before leaving the orchard or woodland, be sure you have only *Glis glis* (photo below),[127] because the wardens have special dormouse-sniffing dogs trained to distinguish between the species. These West Highland White Terriers are uniformed in smart red waistcoats bearing the insignia of the Royal Family, and they take their work seriously.

When you have enough dormice and your catch has been inspected, take them home and confine each dormouse to a dolium and place it in the glirarium. Feed them as much as they will eat at least every two hours. (Don't be offended if they only take one or two bites from each piece of fruit; this wasteful behavior is normal and the reason they are considered such pests in orchards.)

After a month or so, they should be quite chubby. Kill and skin the dormice. Remove and discard the head and tail. Remove the legs; discard the leg bones, but save the leg meat. Through a ventral (the stomach side) midline incision, remove the entrails and discard them. Rinse the carcasses and cover with damp paper towels while you prepare the stuffing. Pre-heat a wood-burning oven to 350°F.

STUFFED DORMOUSE

The earliest known recipe for stuffed dormouse is found in a manuscript entitled De Re Coquinaria, (probably written in the fourth century) and is ascribed to Caelius Apicius.

"Glires:
Isicio porcino, item pulpis ex omni membro glirium trito, cum pipere, nucleis, lasere, liquamine farcies glires et sutos in tegula positos mittes in furnum aut farsos in cilbano coque."

Translation: "Dormice: Stuffed dormice with pork filling, and with the meat of whole dormice ground with pepper, pine nuts, silphium, and garum. Sew up and place on a baking tile, and put them in the oven; or cook the stuffed [dormice] in a pan."

A nearly authentic present-day version would be as follows:

For each dormouse, mix two ounces of sausage meat or ground pork with the chopped dormouse leg and neck meat, two teaspoons of pine nuts, a teaspoon each of finely chopped garlic and fennel root (or one tsp. Indian "hing"), a quarter-teaspoon of garum (piquant fish sauce from Spain) or anchovy paste (or Gentlemen's Relish), and a pinch of black pepper. Blend this mixture briefly in a food processor until it is finely ground, but not so much that it turns into a paste.

Stuff each dormouse with the filling. With a needle and thread, sew up the abdominal musculature at the incision, and pinch the neck and leg holes closed. Brush each dormouse with melted butter, line them up on a pizza tile, stomach side down, and put the tile into the oven. Alternatively, put the dormice in a covered earthenware casserole. Bake them for 25 minutes.

Baked stuffed dormice are delicious served on a bed of rice or mashed potatoes, accompanied by sautéed arugula or broccoli rabe. In the unlikely event that any are leftover, they are wonderful the next day with a pan of bubble and squeak.

Alan White, late editor of *Bandersnatch* (a publication of the British Lewis Carroll Society, Issue 11, April, 2001), notes that the British Minister of Agriculture, Fisheries, and Food issued licenses to trap *Glis glis*, the edible dormouse, only three times in recent years. The results appear in the table below:

Year	Number of dormice taken
1986	4
1987	57
1988	6

ROSES

Roses [128], produced by various species of shrubs of the family Rosaceae and the genus *Rosa*, have been prized for centuries for their alleged medicinal, cosmetic, mythological, and culinary properties. The petals, leaves, and seed pods ("hips") of roses are all edible.

Roses are imbued with an extensive medicinal folklore, which includes their ability to lift depression; cure colds, coughs, infections, itching, acne, headaches, and stomach aches; prevent spider veins; and purify the blood. An impressive repertoire for a single botanical genus!

CHAPTER 8, in which Alice learns to cook with roses and flamingo tongues, and prepares a Gypsy recipe for hedgehogs.

"A large rose-tree stood near the entrance of the garden: the roses growing on it were white, but there were three gardeners at it, busily painting them red. Alice thought this a very curious thing, and she went nearer to watch them..."

Alice had heard of many things that were commonly done with roses, but painting them was not one with which she was familiar. She knew of using rose petals as potpourri, and for making rosewater, and even that they were used in some desserts. Just the thought of dessert made Alice long for something sweet to eat. Knowing that paint must not be good to eat, she snatched several of the unpainted roses before the Queen could notice, and made quickly for the kitchen.

Cosmetic uses of rose preparations include perfuming the body, sweetening the breath, and as a cleansing and astringent agent. Rosewater, in particular, has a long history: It was first mentioned by the poet and physician Nicander in 140 B.C., and much later, in Tudor and Stuart England, was very fashionable for finger bowls. Since spoons were not in regular use until the sixteenth century, and forks not until the seventeenth, one can see how useful this hand-cleansing agent could be! Shakespeare, in *The Taming of the Shrew*, wrote: "Let one attend him with a silver basin/full of Rose water and bestrewed with flowers." [129]

The mythology of roses includes their use in love potions and spells, to induce prophetic dreams, and as an aphrodisiac. It is said that roses planted in the garden will attract fairies (though there is little, if any, empirical evidence for this!). Particular types and colors of roses have been imbued with special meaning; here are some of them:

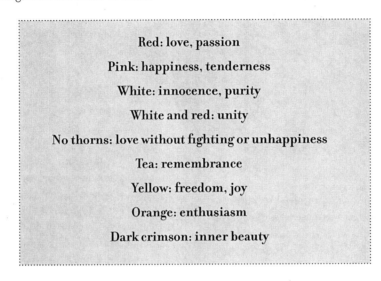

Red: love, passion

Pink: happiness, tenderness

White: innocence, purity

White and red: unity

No thorns: love without fighting or unhappiness

Tea: remembrance

Yellow: freedom, joy

Orange: enthusiasm

Dark crimson: inner beauty

The gift of a single rose indicates that the recipient is special and unique...etc., *ad nauseum*.

The culinary uses for roses are more concrete: Fresh rose petals can be infused into water or vinegar or candied for use as decorations on desserts, and the dried petals can be used to make tea. Rose hips, which are high in Vitamin C, can be used in jams, jellies, syrups, teas, and breads. Needless to say, any parts of a rose to be used in recipes should not be obtained from commercial sources (where the blooms were likely treated with chemicals) or from shrubs that have been sprayed with any noxious chemicals.

rose petal sandwiches

1 sourdough roll	2 leaves of curly Romaine lettuce	10 rose petals
goat cheese	walnuts or pine nuts	red onion slices

"roseberry" dressing (1/2 cup raspberry dressing mixed with 1/2 tsp. rosewater)

Cut roll in half and toast lightly.
Rinse lettuce and rose petals and pat dry.
Place one lettuce leaf on one half of the roll.
Layer rose petals, goat cheese, and nuts.
Top with roseberry dressing.
Place the other lettuce leaf on the other half of the roll, and top with onion slices.
Serve open-faced.[130]

scrambled rose omelet

3 eggs	3 tbs. water	1/4 tsp. rosewater
1/8 cup chives, chopped	1/8 cup feta cheese	4 rose petals
dash of salt	spring of spearmint (for garnish)	

Rinse rose petals, dry them, and cut them into slivers with scissors; set aside.
Separate yolks and whites of eggs into separate bowls.
Add water, rosewater, and salt to egg whites and whisk until blended. Fold in egg yolks and chives and whisk again until blended. Pour into hot, buttered, small omelet pan, and watch for edges to firm. Using a spatula, fold firm edges into center and tip the skillet so that the liquid center runs out to form a new edge; continue until no longer runny, but still wet inside.
Sprinkle cheese and half of the slivered rose petals on top and place in broiler until cheese is lightly melted. Remove pan from broiler and fold omelet in half; transfer to dish and garnish with remaining rose petals and the spearmint.[131]

rose and spearmint tea

1 cup rose petals	1 fresh sprig of spearmint	8 cups boiling water

Rinse rose petals well.
Place in a coffee press with spearmint.
Add boiling water, steep for 3 minutes, press, and serve.
Add one tbs. of honey per cup; optional.[132]

"Alice thought she had never seen such a curious croquet-ground in her life; it was all ridges and furrows; the balls were live hedgehogs, the mallets live flamingoes, and the soldiers had to double themselves up and to stand on their hands and feet, to make the arches…

The chief difficulty Alice found at first was in managing her Flamingo…when she had got its head down, and was going to begin again, it was very provoking to find that the hedgehog had unrolled itself, and was in the act of crawling away…Alice soon came to the conclusion that it was a very difficult game indeed."

The stress of the trying afternoon had made Alice quite hungry again, and as she struggled to control her flamingo, she remembered something her father had told her about flamingos not only being edible, but a delicacy. While the Queen was intent on making her own croquet shot, Alice sneaked away to the kitchen, dragging the unruly flamingo with her.

Alice reached the kitchen without further incident, but immediately realized that she had no idea how to go about cooking the spindly, feathery thing.

FLAMINGOES

And you see, that was *precisely* her problem: she thought she had to cook the *whole* flamingo, for she had obviously forgotten what her father had said long ago about the choicest, most edible part of this beautiful bird, its tongue!

The flamingo, concerned about its tongue…

Alice's father, Dean Liddell, had told her that the bird is named for its red feathers, the Greek word being *phoinikopteros*, which is a compound of *phoinix*, meaning "purplish red," and *pteron*, meaning "wing or feather." The Latin word, *phoenicopterus*, was of course derived from the Greek, as Alice could easily see without even having to check its etymology in her father's large *Greek-English Lexicon*, a standard work curiously difficult to find in Wonderland.

And it was the Romans who became so fond of the taste of the flamingo. The Elder Pliny in his *Naturalis Historia* wrote: "Phoenicopteri linguam praecipui saporis esse Apicius docuit, nepotum omnium altissimus gurges," which means "Apicius taught that the tongue of the flamingo tastes excellent, and he was

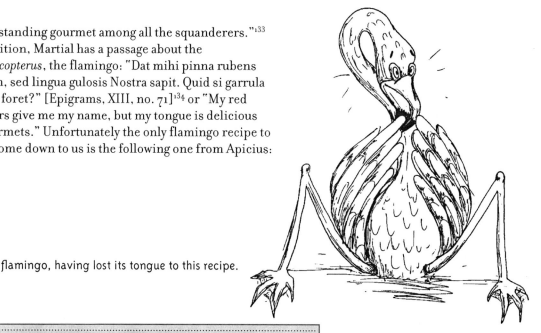

an outstanding gourmet among all the squanderers."[133]
In addition, Martial has a passage about the
phoenicopterus, the flamingo: "Dat mihi pinna rubens
nomen, sed lingua gulosis Nostra sapit. Quid si garrula
lingua foret?" [Epigrams, XIII, no. 71][134] or "My red
feathers give me my name, but my tongue is delicious
to gourmets." Unfortunately the only flamingo recipe to
have come down to us is the following one from Apicius:

The flamingo, having lost its tongue to this recipe.

In PHOEnICOPTEro

{240} Phoenicopterum eliberas, lauas, ornas, includis in
caccabum, adicies aquam, salem, anethum et aceti modicum,
dimidia coctura alligas fasciculum porri et coriandri, ut
coquatur, prope cocturam defritum mittis, coloras, adicies
in mortarium piper, cuminum, coriandrum, laseris radicem,
mentam, rutam, fricabis, suffundis acetum, adicies caryotam,
ius de suo sibiperfundis, reexinanies in eundem caccabum,
amulo obligas, ius perfundis et inferes.{241} Idem facies et in
psittaco.[135]

Roman Roast FLamInGo (Translation)

Pluck your flamingo, wash it, truss it, put it in a pot. Add
water, salt, some dill, and a little vinegar. When half cooked,
tie together a bouquet of leeks and coriander and cook with
the flamingo. When it is almost done, add defrutum for color.
In a mortar place pepper, cumin, coriander, silphium root,
mint, and rue; then grind, moisten with vinegar, add dates
and pour in the broth. Empty into the same pot and thicken
with starch. Pour the sauce over the flamingo and serve. You
may do the same thing with a parrot.

Suetonius mentions that the emperor Vitellius often served flamingo tongues with other exotic dishes:

"In hac scarorum iocinera, phasianorum cerebella, linguas phoenicopterum, muraenarum lactes a Parthia usque fretoque Hispanico per Navarchos ac Trieremes petitiarum commiscuit; hoc est, ab extremis imperii finibus orientem versus et occidentem."[136]

Translated, "In this he mixed together the livers of pikes, the brains of pheasants and peacocks, the tongues of flamingoes, and the milk of lampreys, brought by his naval captains and triremes from the whole empire, from Parthia to the Spanish strait; that is, from the eastern to the western boundaries of the Roman world."

And the later, even more degenerate, emperor Heliogabulus, seems to have been confused and substituted the brains of the flamingo for its tongue at his sumptuous feasts, according to Lampridius: "exhibuit et palatinis lances ingentes extis mullorum refertas et cerebellis phoenicopterum..."[137]

Translated, "He served to the palace attendants, moreover, huge platters heaped with the viscera of mullets and flamingo brains..."

Flamingo tongues (illustration [138]) were an esteemed delicacy because they were "large, having a large knob of fat at the root, which is an excellent bit, and a dish fit for a prince's table."[139]

It is not the tongue of the flamingo but rather its beak that Alice uses as the head of her croquet mallet. In fact, Lewis Carroll may have been inspired to use the flamingo as a natural mallet because of the frequently assumed position of the flamingo in turning over its egg, as in this photo.[140]

In the Bodleian Library, Alice could have found, if she had only looked carefully enough, the recipe for roast flamingo in its original French version, a language with which Alice was already quite familiar, which we easily acquired from the internet; alas, a resource unavailable to Alice.

ROAST SWAN FLAMINGO

Take a swan flamingo and prepare it and put it on to roast until it is all cooked, then make a paste of eggs, as clear as paper, and pour it on the said swan flamingo while turning the spit so that the paste cooks on it, and be careful that no wings or thighs be broken, and put the swan flamingo's neck as though it were swimming in water, and to keep it in this position, you must put a skewer in its head which will rest between the two wings, passing all other, until it holds the neck firm, and another skewer below the wings, and another between the thighs, and another close to the feet and at each foot three to spread the foot: and when it is well cooked and well gilded with the paste, take out the skewers, except that in the neck, then make a terrace of whole wheat pastry, which should be thick and strong, and which is one fist thick, made with nice fluting all around, and let it be two feet long, and a foot and a half broad, or a little more, then cook it without boiling, and have it painted green like a grassy meadow, and gild your swan flamingo with a skin of silver, except for about two fingers width around the neck, which is not gilded, and the beak and the feet, then have a flying cloak, which should be of crimson sendal on the inside, and emblazon the top of said cloak with whatever arms you wish, and around the swan flamingo have banners, the sticks two and a half feet long with banners of sendal, emblazon with whatever arms you wish, and put all in a dish the size and shape of the terrace, and present it to whomever you wish.[141]

"Why are flamingos pink?" Alice might well have asked. Even the great Professor Buckland might not have known that the birds' diet of shrimp and worms from salt ponds gives them their particularly memorable color.[142] It is the carotenoid pigments in the algae eaten by the shrimp that give both the shrimp and flamingos their rosy shades.

Abbott Handerson Thayer had an interesting theory for the bright coloration of flamingos: he believed that their coloring allowed them to blend in with the sunset and sunrise! This theory was based on the principle of countershading, which refers to the underside of an animal's fur, skin, or feathers being a lighter shade than the dorsal ("top") part. Countershading, also called "Thayer's Law," for his 1892 study on the subject, is thought to provide camouflage by reducing conspicuous shadows that might otherwise reveal the silhouette of the animal to a predator. While countershading can be demonstrated in a variety of animal species, including some insects, the flamingo is not one of them. Thayer was ridiculed by his scientific peers for extrapolating his theory to include all fauna. His critics included Theodore Roosevelt, who sent Thayer a derogatory missive on this subject in 1911.[143]

"Flamingo" is the Latin word for flame, probably a reference to its color. Flamingos are filter feeders and eat with their heads upside down. They use an unusual feeding method to capture their food of algae, diatoms, and aquatic invertebrates, such as brine flies, shrimps, and mollusks. Their bills are shaped so that when turned upside down, they act like a sieve, filtering organisms from the water. The bill is fringed on the edges and lined with comb-like structures called lamellae, which help capture the food. The birds put their beaks into the water and use their tongues as pumps to bring water into the beak and then squeeze it out again; essentially, the tongue acts like a piston, expelling water and mud three or four times a second. The brush-like appendages on the tongue collect the food, and when the tongue is moved back to pull more water into the beak, the food can be swallowed.[144]

Having dealt with the flamingo, Alice returned to the croquet lawn, but found that she was still annoyed by the odd way in which this particular game of croquet was played:

" 'I don't think they play at all fairly,' Alice began, in rather a complaining tone,' and they all quarrel so dreadfully one can't hear oneself speak — and they don't seem to have any rules in particular; at least, if there are, nobody attends to them — and you've no idea how confusing it is all the things being alive; for instance, there's the arch I've got to go through next walking about at the other end of the ground — and I should have croqueted the Queen's hedgehog just now, only it ran away when it saw mine coming?' "

Alice was particularly exasperated with the uncooperative hedgehogs, and, of course, all this aggravation made her increasingly hungry. Being a girl bright beyond her years, Alice knew that "hotchi-witchi" was the Romany name by which the Gypsies in Great Britain referred to the hedgehog and also the term for a special dish, a stew made primarily of hedgehogs, beloved by true British Gypsies. As she saw the delectable hedgehogs scurrying around, she thought fondly of the last time she enjoyed hotchi-witchi. In an instant, she had a hedgehog secured in each of her apron pockets, and, avoiding the Queen's gimlet eye, ran to the security of the hedgerow at the edge of the croquet ground, and from there, home and into the kitchen.

HEDGEHOGS

The hedgehog, *Erinaceus europaeus*, is an insectivorous mammal of the family Erinaceidae. It has had a long history in Britain, but it was not always considered a "cute" animal, to be protected in the wild and/or kept as a pet: British Gypsies found it delicious! Gipsy Petulengro, the great historian of Gypsy folklore in the British Isles, preserves the following account of the delicacy known as hotchi-witchi: "As a dish the hotchi-witchi is unrivalled. It is more succulent than a rabbit and more tasty than a pig. Also it does not eat the filth a pig eats; it is clean in its habits, and pure in its food...Once you have caught him...It is really very simple to get a hedgehog to uncurl. You only have to know his weakness. For the hedgehog is like a lady, he loves to be tickled. All you need do is rub your finger or stick up and down his back and he uncurls. The gentlest tap on the nose and he is unconscious. He is not as difficult to skin as you might imagine. You run a red-hot poker over him and burn his spines, hang him on a hook, and take his skin off. Some Romanys prefer to leave him unskinned, roll him in wet clay, rub him in the embers of the fire, and when baked, break the clay, which comes apart with the bristles and skin. This is the best way of keeping the luscious juices intact and the flavour of the meat unimpaired. However, he can be very pleasantly cooked in the simpler way with herbs, particularly agrimony and sorrel which permeate the flesh and are as essential to Romany cooking as is garlic to the Greek or Italian. I well remember once as we sat around the bor-yag eating our hotchi-witchi some gentlemen belonging to a shooting-party on a neighboring estate passed near us and were curious to see what smelt so good. They congratulated us, and added enviously, that their luncheon, which was only pheasant, would not be half as good."[145]

Not all Gypsies, however, were as fond of the hedgehog. George Henry Borrow recounts this anecdote in his account of the Gypsies of Spain: "Know, then, O Gentile, whether thou be from the land of the Gorgios [England] or the Busne [Spain], that the very Gypsies who consider a ragout of snails a delicious dish will not touch an eel, because it bears resemblance to a snake; and that those who will feast on a roasted hedgehog could be induced by no money to taste a squirrel, a delicious and wholesome species of gabe, living in the purest and most nutritious food which the fields and forests can supply. I myself, while living among the Roms of England, have been regarded almost in the light of a cannibal for cooking the latter animal and preferring it to hotchiwitchu barbecued…"[147]

The hedgehog, depicted here in an old engraving,[148] has a place in Gypsy literature as well as in the haute cuisine tradition. Leland preserves the following fable of "The Bird and the Hedgehog:"

> ## GYPSY-STYLE ROAST HEDGEHOG
>
> Enclose the animal in clay and place it on stones made white hot.
>
> When it is cooked, remove the clay (the prickles remain attached to the clay crust) and the entrails. Serve wrapped in large leaves.[146]

"Pre yeck divvs a hotchewitchi diked a chillico adree the puv, and the chillico puckered Iesco, 'Mor jal pauli by the kushto wastus, or the hunters' graias will chiv tute adree the chick, mullo; an' if you jal the waver rikk by the bongo wast, dovo 's a Rommany tan adoi, and the Rommany chals will haw tute.' Penned the hotchewitchi, 'I'd rather jal with the Rommany chals, an' be hawed by foci that daum mandy, than be pirraben apre by chals that dick kaulo apre mandy.' It's kushtier for a tacho rom to mullered by a Rommany pal than to be nashered by the Gorgios."[149]

Translation:

On a day a hedgehog met a bird in the field, and the bird told him, "Do not go around by the right hand or the hunters' horses will trample you dead in the dirt; and if you go around by the left hand, there's a Gypsy tent, and the Gypsies will eat you." Said the hedgehog, "I'd rather go with the Gypsies, and be eaten by folk that like me, than be trampled on by people that look black on me." It is better for a real Gypsy to be killed by a Gypsy brother than to be hung by Gorgios.

There is much truth to that, as little Alice could readily perceive. And she remembered too, though none too clearly, what her father, Dean Liddell, had said to her about the word hedgehog as they saw one rolled up by the side of the road on one of their walks in the country around Oxford. Smart and Crofton, he said, give for hotchi-witchi the following entry: Hotchi-witchi, Hoc'a, epic, pique; hoc'aviça, porc, epine, herisson; hoc'lo, herisse, piquant.[150] [More than a century later the Dean would have been pleased to read the thorough treatment of the word by Boretzky and Igla: Kanzavuri m [kandzuro] 1. Igel, edgehog. 2 Werwolf; werewolf. 3. Spitzbube, Gauner; rogue, rascal. 4. Spaßmacher, Komiker; joker, comic [< gr. σκάντζοχοιρος, vgl. Pers. xarandaz "Stechelschwein".]][151]

Hedgehog, Stechelschwein — can anything be sweeter?

It is a good thing that Alice did not smack her hedgehog on its nose, the most sensitive part of its little body, for that surely would have killed it and she would have been forced to prepare her own hotchi-witchi in Chapter 8, which would not do at all.

The poet John Clare (1793–1864), known as "the Northampton peasant poet," lived with the Gypsies for a time. Apparently, he was familiar with hotchi-witchi, and wrote this verse about the hedgehog's lifestyle, ending with his unfavorable opinion of this Gypsy dish:[152]

John Clare eventually went insane, but it is not known whether his sojourn with the Gypsies, or his ingestion of hotchi-witchi, or both, contributed to his decline.

THE HEDGEHOG

The hedgehog hides beneath the rotten hedge
And makes a great round nest of grass and sedge,
Or in a bush or in a hollow tree;
And many often stoop and say they see
Him roll and fill his prickles full of crabs
And creep away; and where the magpie dabs
His wing at muddy dyke, in aged root
He makes a nest and fills it full of fruit,
On the hedge bottom hunts for crabs and sloes
And whistles like a cricket as he goes.
It rolls up like a ball or shapeless hog
When gipsies hunt it with their noisy dog;
I've seen it in their camps — they call it sweet,
Though black and bitter and unsavory meat
But they who hunt the fields for rotten meat
And wash in muddy dyke and call it sweat
And eat what dogs refuse whey ere they dwell
Care little either for the taste or smell
They say they milk the cows and when they lye
Nibble their fleshy teats and make them dry
But hey whove seen the small head like a hog
Rolled up to meet the savage of a dog
With mouth scarce big enough to hold a straw
Will neer believe what no one ever saw
But still they hunt the hedges all about
And shepherd dogs are trained to hunt them out
they hurl with savage force the stick and stone
And no one cares and still the strife goes on.

There is a type of dessert known as a "hedgehog;" there is also a savory sausage dish by the same name. These dishes get their names from the general form of the animal, and the appearance of its spines, rather than the flavor of the meat. Each is shaped into an oblong, and then studded with almonds, as the "spines."

(The authors believe that this is far tastier than the real thing!)

APPLE HEDGEHOG

12 middling-sized cooking apples

rind of half a lemon, minced very fine

3 tbs. caster sugar

1/2 pound sugar

2 egg white

whole blanched almonds

1/2 pint water

Peel and core 6 of the apples without dividing them, and stew them very gently with the sugar and water until tender, then lift them carefully on to a dish. Have ready the remainder of the apples peeled, cored, and cut into thin slices; put them into the cooking syrup with the lemon peel, and boil gently until they are reduced to a mashed consistency; they must be kept stirred to prevent them from burning. Cover the bottom of a dish with some of the mashed apples, and place 4 of the stewed apples on top of them; inside and between each place more mashed apples; then put the other 2 whole apples on top, and fill up the cavities as before, forming the whole into a raised oval shape. Whip the whites of the eggs to a stiff froth, mix with them the caster sugar, and cover the apples very smoothly all over with the mixture; cut each almond into 4 or 5 strips, and place these strips at equal distances over the icing, sticking up; strew over a little more sugar, and place the dish in a very cool oven, to color the almonds and to warm the apples through.[153]

SAUSAGE HEDGEHOGS

2 pounds ground pork

1 tsp. sugar

2 tsp. ginger

2 ounces almonds, blanched and slivered

1 tsp. salt

Mix pork and spices to form into balls 1 1/2 to 2 inches in diameter; then elongate the balls a little, into ovals about the size of walnuts. Insert almonds (which may be toasted first) into the "hedgehogs" in a pattern suggesting quills, about 8 almond slivers per "hedgehog." Bake on a cookie sheet at 350°F for about 30 minutes, until golden brown.[154]

Gipsy Petulengro highly recommends hedgehog fat as a cure for deafness: "Melt the fat and pour a drop into the ear at night. This relieves the ear drum and dissolves the hard wax which is a frequent cause of deafness. This is a fine old Gypsy remedy. Many obstinate cases of deafness have been overcome by this treatment. I cured myself thus when I had a bad attack of deafness some years ago. People who are what is often called 'a little hard of hearing' should try this remedy without delay. It will possibly save them from going in time completely deaf."[155]

Dr. Thomas Muffett, in 1575, also recommended ingestion of the hedgehog, as it "nourisheth plentifully, procureth appetite and sleep, strengthening Travailers, preserveth women with child from miscarrying, disolveth knots and kernelly tumors, help the Lepry, consumption, Palsy, Dropsie, Stone, and Convulsion."[156] An impressive array of benefits from a single species!

"Your father the Dean [Buckland]," Lord Playfair writes to Mrs. Gordon, "was a born experimentalist, and I recollect various queer dishes which he had at his table. The hedgehog was a successful experiment, and both Liebig and I thought it good and tender. On another occasion I recollect a dish of crocodile, which was an utter failure. The Dean's experiment in quaint gastronomy used to remind me of the dinner on garden snails at which Black, Hutton and Playfair determined to get over their natural prejudice; but though the three philosophers took one mouthful; they could not be persuaded to swallow it, and rejected the morsel with strong language. The crocodile at your father's table had a similar fate."[157]

TURTLES

Green sea turtles (*Chelonia mydas*), collected on voyages to the New World, could be kept alive on board ship, and provided fresh meat on the three-month return trip. When surviving turtles reached Europe, royalty quickly developed an appetite for the meat, and soup made from it became very fashionable in Victorian England. (The soup often contained the turtle's eggs as well as the meat.) However, many who aspired to this social height could not afford real turtle meat, and veal (often a calf's

CHAPTER 9, in which Alice encounters turtles (both real and mock), learns of the singing Fijian princess, and is introduced to the *Ambulocetus*.

head) was substituted. This less costly "mock turtle" soup became popular at middle-class parties and restaurants. Mock turtle soup was served on special occasions at Christ Church, Oxford, which may explain Tenniel's depiction of Carroll's mock turtle as an animal with bovine head, legs, and tail, but a chelonian body and front flippers.

"*Then the Queen left off, quite out of breath, and said to Alice, 'Have you seen the Mock Turtle yet?'*

'No,' said Alice. 'I don't even know what a Mock Turtle is.'

'It's the thing Mock Turtle Soup is made from,' said the Queen.

'I never saw one, or heard of one,' said Alice.

'Come on, then,' said the Queen, 'and he shall tell you his history'... They very soon came upon a Gryphon, lying fast asleep in the sun... 'Up, lazy thing!' said the Queen, 'and take this young lady to see the Mock Turtle, and to hear his history...'

So they went up to the Mock Turtle, who looked at them with large eyes full of tears, but said nothing...

'Once,' said the Mock Turtle at last, with a deep sigh, 'I was a real Turtle.' "

By the time Alice had heard the Mock Turtle's extensive account of his life history, she was more than ready for some elevenses. She had become damp and chilly, sitting for so long on the seashore, and she thought that some soup would do quite nicely — Mock Turtle Soup! She was faced with a dilemma, though: If the main ingredient was to be "mock" turtle, and so was not TURTLE at all, then what WAS it? Alice went to the Department of Fisheries for help. The officials there were happy to explain the regulations governing the consumption of turtles. Although she was by then well-informed on which real turtle species could (and could not) be caught legally and eaten, no one could tell her what to use as mock turtle in her soup. As she was absently making her way back through the village, she came upon the solution: Use the REAL Mock Turtle! She passed back near the shingle where the Quadrille was still in progress, and invited the Mock Turtle to accompany her home. She was then able to persuade him to step out of his shell and jump into the nice warm soup pot.

In North America, the green sea turtle was added to the Endangered Species List in 1970, cutting off one source of meat for turtle soup. The alligator snapping turtle (*Macroclemys temminkii*, another favored delicacy) was considered "vulnerable" as of 2002, and is protected in all states except Louisiana, where they are known as *cowans* and are prized for soup. It is said that meat from different parts of a turtle's body can have as many as seven different flavors (rather like Heinz pickles!), and this belief may have added to its culinary appeal.[58] It is commonly thought that commercially available alligator snapper meat comes from farm-raised animals, but that, unfortunately, is not always the case.[59]

Two conservation biologists, Joe Roman, of Harvard University, and Brian Bowen, at the University of Florida, are turtle meat "detectives" who collect samples of "turtle meat" from restaurants, seafood markets, turtle farms, rendering plants, and from the internet, and compare the DNA of each sample to a database they developed for several reptilian and other meat-animal species. The biologists' observations[60] of alligator snapping turtles (a favorite for soup) show that each population of the turtles (whose habitats are restricted to the large gulf draining rivers of southeastern United States) has evolved in separate river habitats in virtual isolation over many generations, and so has its own unique genetic "footprint." The DNA tests reveal whether the sample originated from legally harvested turtles, or from endangered and protected species (or, even, whether the meat is actually any type of turtle meat!). Thus, turtles taken from different river environments can be identified, and poachers punished.

While Roman and Bowen found no meat sample that contained green sea turtle, they did identify meat from other turtles, namely, the soft-shell turtle and common snapping turtle. The only sample of alligator snapper they collected was provided by a shopkeeper who (in front of a "decoy" pen of common snappers) told the biologists that it was illegal to sell the meat of alligator snappers. More than a quarter of the thirty-four samples tested were not from any species of turtle at all! The meat of the American alligator, which can be legally obtained from farm-raised alligators, or those hunted in season, and pork, are often used as "mock turtle." Because the meat is ground, identification by visual or taste inspection is difficult. Conservation and genetic biologists estimate that 25-30% of luxury wildlife meat items are falsely labeled. This substitution of a commoner, cheaper wildlife species for a scarcer, more desirable, and more expensive one has been termed "the mock turtle syndrome," in "honor" (a dubious one, to be sure!) of Lewis Carroll.

When we examine recipes for mock turtle soup, there seem to be endless variations in the primary ingredients. One recipe calls for veal, fishcakes, and sherry; another for beef cubes, onions, celery, peppers, and chopped hard-boiled eggs; yet another specifies a calf's head and vegetables! It seems that mock turtle can be prepared from any ingredients *except* turtle, thereby making a mockery of these recipes.

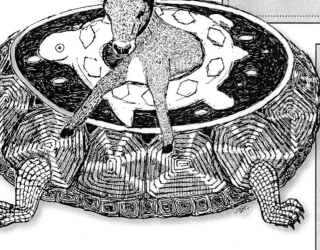

MOCK TURTLE SOUP (1)

2 pounds lean shin of beef
1/2 calf's head (the lower half)

1 onion	1 carrot	1 turnip
1 bouquet garni	2 or 3 cloves	1 blade or pinch of mace
1 tbs. butter	1 tbs. flour	1 small glass sherry

salt and pepper

Using a sharp knife, remove all meat from shin of beef. Soak the calf's head in salted cold water for a hour after having it boned. Tie the bones in a piece of muslin. Place the calf's head, rolled and tied up, and beef and beef bones in 2-3 quarts of cold water, and add 2 tbs. of rock salt. Bring gently to the boiling point, skim well, then add half the onion, the carrot, turnip, bouquet garni, mace, cloves, and a few peppercorns. Cover closely and allow to simmer gently for 4 hours; then strain and set to cool. When cold remove every speck of fat from surface.

Melt the butter in a frying pan, add the rest of the onion, sliced, and fry brown; add the flour, browning it also, then moisten with some of the stock, and add to the rest of the soup, which as been reheated to the boiling point. When the soup slightly thickens, withdraw the pan from the fire, add sherry, season to taste and garnish with the diced meat from the calf's head and small pieces of the lean beef.[161]

MOCK TURTLE SOUP (2)

Simmer some large presoaked pigs' ears in water overnight with a clove-stuck onion, a bunch of herbs (marjoram, basil, and thyme), and a little vinegar. Allow to cool. Skim off fat and remove and skin the ears. Cut them into thin strips. Strain the stock through muslin and reduce it well over a brisk heat. Season it with mace, white pepper, salt, lemon juice, and a glass of sherry. Add the ear strips and serve hot.[162]

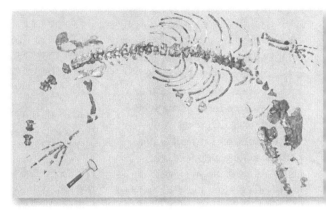

The mock turtle has been the subject of anecdotes originating from various cultures; here is one: "Along the banks of the Ohio River, between the Mill Creek and the Miami River tributaries, is the habitat of the mock turtle. Early German settlers to the region found this creature to be an excellent component for their beloved old-world *Schildkrötesuppe* (turtle soup). However, the mock turtle is a cagey critter, more so than the *Reißenschildkröte* (Giant Turtle) of the Rhine, and frequently eluded its Teutonic pursuers. The Germans, embarrassed to admit that they could be outwitted by an amphibian [sic; a turtle is a reptile, not an amphibian], attributed its elusiveness to speed, and called their prized quarry (on the rare occasions they came home with one) "very fast turtle" or *Machschildkröte*, from which we get "mock turtle." Today, the mock turtle is endangered, and thus is not available commercially. However, the uniquely sweet-sour flavor of the mock turtle is closely approximated with the correct combination of hamburger, lemon, brains, ketchup, and vinegar. (A brainless recipe is also provided for Midwesterners who are having trouble finding any.)"[163]

Given the odd nature and anatomy of Tenniel's rendition of the Mock Turtle (a sort of mammal-reptile with ungulate feet), one might consider the hypothesis that it represents an intermediate animal form, hitherto unrecorded in the fossil record. One might even entertain the notion that the Mock Turtle may have some relation to the forty-nine million year old Archaeocete, recently discovered by J.G.M. Thewissen[164, 165] in a Pakistani cave; he named it *Ambulocetus natans*. This animal was ten to twelve feet long, with a skull a yard long, and weighed about six hundred fifty pounds. Above is Prof. Thewissen's photograph of the disarticulated skeleton, shown in relation to the size of an ordinary sledge hammer.[166]

This animal (and similar species, one of which was known as *Andrewsarchus*) has been described as "a furry crocodile,"[167] and more ferociously, as "a cross between an alligator and an Alsatian on steroids."[168]

Ambulocetus natans, crude rendering by author A.C.T.

Ambulocetus had a large, elongated head with strong jaws and large teeth, four legs that could support its weight on land, and a long tail. At the distal end of each leg, there were small hooves on each toe, much like the Mock Turtle's. *Ambulocetus* was an excellent swimmer and hunted prey by ambush; it held prey underwater until dead, and could ingest very large animals. This transitional fossil is closely related to the modern whale; Thewissen states that "*Ambulocetus* represents a critical intermediate between land mammals and marine cetaceans."[169]

> " 'Oh, you sing,' said the Gryphon. 'I've forgotten the words.'
>
> And the Mock Turtle began to sing 'Will you walk a little faster, said a whiting to a snail.' "

TURTLE CALLERS

This was really rather a reversal of things, for Alice quite well remembered having heard of those young virgins, the turtle callers of the Fiji Islands, who sing to the turtles to call them up and so thought she would have to sing to the turtle. Many years later, Christopher Venning described the quaint practice of girls singing to South Sea turtles, and recounted the turtle singing ceremony on the coast of the Fijian island of Vunisea in this way:

"There is an old Fijian legend which tells of the capture of a Fijian princess by a young prince who had fallen in love with her. All her life she had three turtles as companions, and anyone kidnapping her had to kidnap the turtles too. This was done one day, but as soon as the turtles were landed in the boat they managed, by some magic powers, to dissolve and trickle into the water. Although the princess was taken away her three turtles have remained to this day, and for some reason, respond when they hear this chant calling them. However, the turtle women of Vunisea settled themselves on top of the rock and began a mournful chant which they repeated over and over again. After a while, as we gazed at the water far below us, three brownish forms slowly came to the surface, three turtles which stayed there for quite a while before gradually drifting away. How the women started calling them, or why they came, no one could explain."[170]

Of course, the Fijian princess' turtles turned themselves into turtle soup. Any species turning itself into soup is a magical occurrence whenever and wherever it happens. Even if it turns out to be mock turtle soup!

LOBSTERS

The lobster (*Homarus americanus* in North America, and *Homarus gammarus* in northern Europe, including the British Isles) is a popular and elegant menu item. These cold-water decapods are bottom-dwellers and hunt for small crustaceans, but are scavengers as well. They are also aggressive cannibals, preying on the young of their own species.

Lobsters live in shallow, rocky areas near the shore. They have the ability to regenerate lost claws, legs and antennae, and can even "amputate" their own claws and legs in order to escape danger. Lobsters are nocturnal, hiding in rock crevices by day, and coming out to feed at night. They are easily caught in traps (lobster "pots") baited with fish scraps.

Recent scientific evidence shows that lobsters, which normally travel significant distances each night in foraging for food, possess the ability to

CHAPTER 10, in which Alice meets the vanilla lobster and encounters fish that are served with their tails in their mouths.

use true navigation; i.e., the capacity to determine their positions relative to a geographic point without having viewed the route in advance. The experiments involved taking lobsters from their normal environment and loading them onto a boat, in closed boxes, that deliberately traveled a circuitous route. The lobsters, tethered and with

" 'You may not have lived much under the sea — ' (I haven't,' said Alice) —'and perhaps you were never even introduced to a lobster —' (Alice began to say 'I once tasted — ' but checked herself hastily, and said 'No, never') ' — so you can have no idea what a delightful thing a Lobster Quadrille is!'

'No, indeed,' said Alice. 'What sort of a dance is it?'

'Why,' said the Gryphon, 'you first form into a line along the sea-shore —'

' —you advance twice —'

'Each with a lobster as a partner!' cried the Gryphon...

' —change lobsters, and retire in same order,' continued the Gryphon.

'Then, you know,' the Mock Turtle went on, 'you throw the —'

'The lobsters!' shouted the Gryphon, with a bound into the air.

' —as far out to sea as you can —'

'Swim after them!' screamed the Gryphon. "

After several strenuously executed figures of the Lobster Quadrille, Alice was definitely ready for a substantial meal. She was inspired by the enthusiasm of her new friends for the delicious decapods (although they had motives quite different from hers!), and wondered whether throwing perfectly good lobsters out to sea made very good sense... Alice decided that it did not, and went off (surreptitiously, so that the others would not notice and become offended) in search of a couple of lobsters that might not have been thrown quite far enough, and found two that had landed conveniently on the shingle. She had them clip their claws onto the gathers of her dress, where they were well-concealed beneath her apron. She then made her way quickly to the kitchen and set about preparing the lobsters.

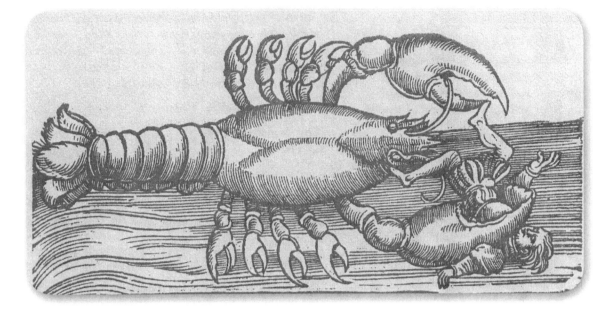

their eyes covered, were then released and their movements monitored. With few exceptions, the lobsters began walking in the correct direction towards "home." Further testing with deliberately erroneous magnetic fields confirmed the results that lobsters use the magnetic properties of the earth to navigate.[171]

Early civilizations apparently appreciated the lobster (depicted in the woodcut, above)[172] as much as we do: The Romans portrayed lobsters, along with other edible sea creatures, on mosaic floors that formed part of domestic and public decoration.[173]

Lobsters are usually prepared for human consumption by steaming or broiling; they may be eaten hot, or the cold, dissected meat can be used in salads and sandwiches.

LOBSTER WITH VANILLA BUTTER SAUCE

8 tbs. unsalted butter

2 shallots (1 1/2 ounces), finely diced

2/3 cup dry white wine

1 tbs. white wine vinegar

1 vanilla bean (4 inches long), split lengthwise and pulp scraped out

kosher or sea salt

freshly ground black pepper

2 live 1 3/4 pound hard-shell lobsters

Position a rack in the broiler so that the lobsters will be 6 to 8 inches from the heating element. Preheat the broiler. Put 2 tbs. butter in a small saucepan (1 quart).

Cut the remaining butter into 1/2 inch cubes and set aside.

Add the shallots to the pan and cook over low to medium heat for about 2 minutes, just until light brown. Add the white wine and vinegar and turn the heat to medium-high. Boil until just 3 to 4 tsp. of liquid remain. Remove the pan from the heat and add the vanilla bean pulp. Return the pan to low heat. Whisk the cubes of butter, a few at a time, into the reduction. Move the saucepan on and off the heat as needed to maintain a temperature of about 180°F; do not boil. When all the butter has been whisked into the sauce, season it with salt and pepper. The sauce should be silky smooth and pale yellow with specks of vanilla. Keep it warm while you prepare the lobster.

Split the lobsters in half lengthwise. Remove and discard the head sac and intestine. Remove the tomalley and the roe if present and place in a small bowl, and break into pieces with a fork. With the back of a knife, crack the center of each claw on one side only. Arrange the lobsters on a broiler pan so that they do not overlap. Divide the tomalley and roe among the cavities and season lightly with salt and pepper.

The lobster, dressed in vanilla beans, its head adorned with the orchid that is the flower of the vanilla vine.

Lightly brush the lobsters all over with the vanilla butter sauce. Broil for 5 minutes. Remove the pan and quickly baste the lobsters with the sauce. Reverse the pan and return it to the broiler for 5 more minutes (total cooking time, 11 minutes, or until the tail meat is creamy white). Keep the butter sauce warm. If it seems too thick, thin it with a few drops of water.

Remove the lobsters from the broiler and lightly brush the lobsters with the sauce one last time. Serve immediately with the remaining sauce poured into small bowls or ramekins for dipping.[174]

"'Oh, as to the whiting,' said the Mock Turtle, 'they — you've seen them, of course?'

'Yes,' said Alice, 'I've often seen them at dinn —' she checked herself hastily.

'I don't know where Dinn may be,' said the Mock Turtle, 'but if you've seen them so often, of course you know what they're like.'

'I believe so,' Alice replied thoughtfully. 'They have their tails in their mouths — and they're all over crumbs.'

'You're wrong about the crumbs,' said the Mock Turtle: 'crumbs would all wash off in the sea. But they HAVE their tails in their mouths…'"

Even after devouring her lobsters, Alice was still a little hungry; she had not realized just how much of a lobster was shell! "Whiting might serve nicely as a second course," she thought. However, she then recalled very clearly that the breaded whiting she had been served at home was mushy, tasteless, and uninspired. On her way to the fishmonger's, she planned a new recipe that would definitely kick the whiting up a notch.

WHITING

Many fish species of the family Gadidae (including hake and pollock) are called "whiting," but the fish known in America as the true "English whiting" is *Merlangius merlangus*. It is common in the North Sea and parts of the Atlantic Ocean. (Just to confuse the issue, American fish species called "whiting" are actually members of the Sciaenidae, the "croaker" family, and are related to spots, sea trout, and drum.) Prior to the twentieth century, English whiting was considered a poor quality fish, fit as food only for the poor and for pets. However, with fishing harvests steadily declining, whiting has come to be valued more highly. Mature whiting may attain weights of more than six pounds,[175] but most are caught commercially at considerably smaller sizes. Whiting taste best when caught from November to March, but may be eaten at any time of year. The flesh of whiting is virtually tasteless, and takes on the flavor of other ingredients with which the fish is cooked. Whiting are often served with their tails between their teeth, a presentation for which there is actually a French culinary term that is taken from the taxonomic name: *Merlan en colere*.

CHAPTER TEN

WHITING STUFFED WITH PRAWNS

4 whiting fillets
1/2 pounds small shrimp, peeled, deveined, and briefly boiled with a bay leaf and several peppercorns
1 medium onion, diced
6 ounces mushrooms, cleaned and diced
3 tbs. butter, divided   3/4 cup fine breadcrumbs   salt and pepper to taste

Saute the onion and mushrooms in 2 tbs. of the butter until soft but not browned. Add the shrimp, and salt and pepper to taste. Divide the onion/mushroom/shrimp mixture among the 4 whiting fillets, and spread the mixture out onto the fillets. Roll the fillets and stand on end in a small buttered baking dish. Sprinkle the bread crumbs on top of the fish rolls, and dot with the remaining 1 tbs. butter. Bake in a 325F oven for 20 minutes.[176]

Southern Americans believe that whiting (illustration [177]) is best served fried, but the British have other ideas that generally involve overcooking and heavy sauces. However, here is one historic British whiting recipe that is quite light:

WHITING AUX FINES HERBES

6 small whiting   1 bunch of sweet herbs chopped fine   butter

Clean and skin the fish, fasten the tails in the mouths, and lay them in a baking dish. Mince the herbs very fine, strew them over the fish, and place small pieces of butter over; cover the dish, and let them cook in a moderate oven for 15 to 20 minutes. Turn the fish once or twice, and serve with the butter and herbs poured over.[178]

BLACK PEPPER

Black pepper (*Piper nigrum*) has long been considered the most important spice, in part because it can be stored for many years without loss of pungency. It is native to Malabar, a region on the western coast of southern India, but has been cultivated for millennia; three thousand year old Sanskrit literature mentions pepper. Pepper (illustration [179]) reached Southeast Asia more than two thousand years ago and has been cultivated in Malaysia and Indonesia since about that time.

In 80 B.C., Alexandria, Egypt, was considered the greatest spice trading port of the eastern Mediterranean area; one of its entrances

CHAPTER 11, in which Alice is bombarded with the natural and social histories of black pepper.

was known as "Pepper Gate." In 410 A.D., when Rome was captured, Alaric the Visigoth demanded three thousand pounds of pepper as ransom, and extracted from the Romans a "tax" of another three hundred pounds per year thereafter. Black pepper was one of the earliest items traded between Asia and Europe. In 1101, victorious Genovese soldiers were each given two pounds of pepper as a gift for their successful Palestinian conquest.

In the Middle Ages, Europeans often used pepper to pay rent, dowries, and taxes. It is

"The King and Queen of Hearts were seated on their throne when they arrived…near the King was the White Rabbit, with a trumpet in one hand, and a scroll of parchment in the other. In the very middle of the court was a table, with a large dish of tarts upon it…

'Herald, read the accusation!' said the King.

On this the White Rabbit blew three blasts on the trumpet, and then unrolled the parchment scroll, and read as follows:

'The Queen of Hearts, she made some tarts,
All on a summer day:
The Knave of Hearts, he stole those tarts,
And took them quite away!'

…The next witness was the Duchess' cook. She carried the pepper-box in her hand, and Alice guessed who it was, even before she got into the court, by the way the people near the door began sneezing all at once.

'Give your evidence,' said the King… 'What are tarts made of?'

'Pepper, mostly,' said the cook."

Alice found this quite confusing. She had never heard of tarts being made of pepper, or even having pepper as one of the minor ingredients. She had heard of a dish called Antigua Pepper Pot, though, which she thought must involve quite a bit of pepper. As it was now well past lunchtime, and the sight of the plate of tarts displayed in the courtroom had made her very hungry, Alice thought the Pepper Pot recipe might be a good thing to try. When the King, and more important, the Cook, wasn't looking, she snatched the very substantial pepper-box from the Cook's hand, and ran out of the courtroom.

said that the cities of Alexandria, Genoa, and Venice owed their economic success to the pepper trade. The need for pepper inspired Spanish exploration and spice trade in the fifteenth century.

In 1797, Captain Jonathan Carnes of Salem, Massachusetts, returned from Sumatra with first large pepper cargo and brought the United States into the world spice trade.

In the last decades of the twentieth century, pepper production increased dramatically as new plantations were founded in Thailand, Vietnam, China, and Sri Lanka. In the New World, Brazil is the only important producer, and pepper plantations there were established in the 1930s. However, the most important pepper producers are India and Indonesia, which together account for about 50% of the world production volume.

ANTIGUA PEPPER POT

6 ounces salt pork or thick bacon, chopped

1/2 pound boneless, lean pork, cubed

2 large onions, chopped   10 okra pods

2 pounds callaloo or spinach, washed, and stems removed

4 cups beef or chicken broth   2 tsp. fresh thyme leaves

1 bird chile or 1/2 Scotch bonnet pepper, seeds and veins removed; chopped

2 cloves garlic, chopped   1 tsp. ground black pepper

Brown the salt pork or bacon and the fresh pork together in a skillet. Remove and drain the meat, reserving the fat in the pan. Add the okra and sear over medium-high heat; remove and reserve. Saute the onions in the meat fat until golden. Place all ingredients in a saucepan or Dutch oven. Bring to a boil, then reduce heat and simmer until the meat is tender (about two hours). This can be cooked ahead and reheated; makes 6 servings.[182]

Black pepper comes from the berries of the vine *Piper nigrum*. They are picked approximately nine months after the plant flowers (while the berries are still unripe). The pepper berries are allowed to ferment, and are then sun-dried until they shrivel and turn nearly black. (This is true pepper, and should not be confused with paprika, cayenne pepper, chili pepper, red pepper, and bell pepper, which are fruits from the capiscum family.) Black pepper has a sharp, penetrating aroma and a characteristic woody, piney flavor, and a hot and biting taste. Black pepper is widely used in almost all cuisines of the world, and is particularily popular for comparatively mild stews as preferred in the cuisine of the British Royal Court.[180]

For chemically-oriented readers: Black pepper contains about 3% essential oil, whose aroma is dominated (to a maximum of 80%) by monoterpene hydrocarbons: sabinene, β-pinene, limonene, terpinene, α-pinene, myrcene, Δ3-carene and monoterpene derivatives (borneol, carvone, carvacrol, 1,8-cineol, linalool). Sesquiterpenes make up about 20% of the essential oil: β-caryophyllene, humulene, β-bisabolone and caryophyllene oxide and ketone. Phenylethers (eugenol, myristicin, safrole) are found in traces. Loss of monoterpenes due to bad storage conditions (especially for ground pepper) should be avoided. The most important odorants organoleptically in black pepper are linalool, α-phellandrene, limonene, myrcene and α-pinene; furthermore, branched-chain aldehydes were found (3-methylbutanal, methylpropanal). The pungent principle in pepper is an alkaloid-analog compound, piperine. It is the amide of 5-(2,4-dioxymethylene-phenyl)-hexa-2,4-dienoic acid (piperinic acid) with azinane (piperidine); only the *trans, trans* conformation contributes to pepper's pungency.[181]

COURT CAKES

This chapter concludes the cookbook, and, as the characters have now somehow been restored to their original functional forms (*see Animals = Meals, below*), we will concentrate here on desserts which may (or may not) be (loosely) related to the characters in this chapter. One of these is King Cake, a special pastry used at New Orleans Mardi Gras celebrations. This tradition dates back to twelfth century France, where it was originally a part of the celebration of the feast of Epiphany. The French who settled in Louisiana continued the tradition, where it acquired a Spanish touch with the placing of a "prize" inside the cake. The person who discovered the prize in his/her piece of cake was designated as "King" or "Queen" for the day. The prize could be anything;

CHAPTER 12, in which Alice learns to distinguish king cake from queen cake, receives a lesson in cardiac anatomy, and is introduced to sotelties and warners.

e.g., a coin, a pecan, a bean, or a pea, but since the 1930s, the symbol used has been a small plastic baby, possibly to represent the baby Jesus. The person who finds the baby and becomes "royalty" is obligated to purchase the cake the next year.

King Cake is shaped more or less like a crown, to represent the Three Kings. It is made of a rich "Danish" dough, and iced in "Mardi Gras" colors: Purple represents justice, green signifies faith, and gold indicates power. These three colors

"'What do you know about this business?' the King said to Alice.

'Nothing,' said Alice.

'Nothing WHATEVER?' persisted the King.

'Nothing whatever,' said Alice."

As it happens, Alice knew quite a LOT about "this business." She had, in fact, *devoured* many of the animals in the story!

"The King turned pale, and shut his note-book hastily.

'Consider your verdict,' he said to the jury, in a low, trembling voice..."

Meanwhile, the White Rabbit, which Alice had consumed in a dish she prepared in Chapter 2, had mysteriously reappeared, apparently intact, and was in the courtroom, speaking!

" 'There's more evidence to come yet, please your Majesty,' said the White Rabbit, jumping up in a great hurry; 'this paper has just been picked up.'

'If any one of them can explain it,' said Alice,.... 'I'll give him sixpence. I don't believe there's an atom of meaning in it.' "

And Alice was right; there was no proof that she had eaten any of the animals, and they had suddenly and inexplicably reappeared, in apparent good health, in the courtroom. The King seemed relieved to be able to confirm this:

" 'Why, there they are!' said the King triumphantly, pointing to " all of the lively and vocal animals in the jury box. The only characters that had not regained their normal appearance and activity were the cards; they seemed to have turned into sotelties, and were now, quite surprisingly, made of brightly colored marzipan!

continue a tradition begun in 1872, when they appeared on a Krewe of Rex carnival flag that was especially designed for the visiting Grand Duke of Russia, who came to New Orleans for the carnival that year.[183]

KING CAKE

1/4 cup butter or margarine	1 16-ounce carton sour cream	1/3 cup sugar
1 tsp. salt	1 packages dry yeast	1 tbs. sugar
1/2 cup warm water (105° to 115°F)	2 eggs	1/2 cup sugar
1 1/2 tsp. ground cinnamon	6 to 6 1/2 cups all-purpose flour, divided	
1/3 cup butter or margarine, softened		
Colored sugars (see below)	Colored frostings (see below)	

Combine the first 4 ingredients in a saucepan; heat until butter melts, stirring occasionally. Let mixture cool to 105°F to 115°F.

Dissolve yeast and 1 tbs. sugar in warm water in a large bowl; let stand 5 minutes. Add butter mixture, eggs, and 2 cups of flour; beat at medium speed with an electric mixer for 2 minutes or by hand until smooth. Gradually stir in enough remaining flour to make a soft dough.

Turn dough out onto a lightly floured surface, and knead until smooth and elastic (about 10 minutes). Place in a well-greased bowl, turning to grease top. Cover and let rise in a warm place free from drafts, for 1 hour or until dough is doubled in bulk. Combine 1/2 cup sugar and cinnamon; set aside.

Pinch dough down and divide it in half. Turn one portion of dough out onto a lightly floured surface, and roll to a 28 inch x 10 inch rectangle. Spread half of the butter and half of the cinnamon mixture on the rolled out dough. Roll dough, jelly roll fashion, starting at the long side. Gently place dough roll, seam side down, on a lightly greased baking sheet. Bring ends of dough together and form an oval ring. If you have access to a tiny plastic baby, tuck it into the seam before you seal it. If not, use a large, dried bean. Moisten and pinch the edges together to seal. Repeat this procedure with the second half of the dough.

Cover and let rise in a warm place, free from drafts, 20 minutes or until doubled in bulk.

Bake at 375°F for 15 to 20 minutes or until golden. Decorate each cake with bands of colored frostings, and sprinkle with colored sugars.

COLORED SUGARS

1 1/2 cups sugar, divided

1 to 2 drops each of green, yellow, red and blue food coloring

Combine 1/2 cup sugar and a drop of green coloring in a jar. Place lid on jar, and shake vigorously to evenly mix the color with sugar. Repeat with each color, combining red and blue for purple.

COLORED FROSTINGS

3 cups sifted powdered sugar

3 tbs. butter or margarine, melted

3 to 5 tbs. milk   1/4 tsp. vanilla extract

1 to 2 drops each green, yellow, red, and blue food coloring

Combine powdered sugar and melted butter. Add milk (room temperature) to reach desired consistency for drizzling; stir in vanilla. Divide frosting into 3 batches, tinting one with green, one with yellow, and combining blue and red for purple frosting. Makes about 1 1/2 cups.[184]

Unlike King Cake, Queen Cake (or Queen Elizabeth Cake) has nothing whatsoever to do with Mardi Gras. Compared to the specific and well-recorded history of the King Cake, the origin of Queen Cake is quite a mystery, and it seems that no one really knows much of anything about it. Legend has it that the recipe, and others similar to it, was so named because it was a favorite of the Queen Mother, and it is known that the recipe for it was passed out to fundraising groups during World War II. However, the Palace maintains that: a. The Queen Mother never gave out "favorite" recipes (due to the volume of requests she apparently received), and b. The recipe did not originate either at Buckingham Palace or at Clarence House. Thus, it has been recommended that the cake be called, simply, "Date and Walnut Cake," with no reference whatsoever made to the Queen Mother. We regret that because the name "Queen Cake" suits the purposes of this chapter of our cookbook, we will respectfully disregard that admonition, and continue to use the traditional appellation. (Another name for this type of cake, with its characteristic broiled topping, was "Lazy Daisy," but that name does not relate to this chapter, either!)[185]

> ### QUEEN CAKE
> 2/3 cup butter 2 cups flour (scant)
> 1/4 tsp. baking soda 6 egg whites
> 1 1/4 cups powdered sugar
> 1 1/2 tsp. lemon juice
>
> Cream the butter, add flour gradually, mixed and sifted with soda, then add lemon juice. Beat whites of eggs until stiff; add sugar gradually, and combine the mixtures. Bake 50 minutes in a long shallow pan. Cover with caramel frosting, or broiled topping. [186]

queen ELIZABETH cake

1 cup boiling water
1 cup dates, chopped
1 tsp. baking soda
1/2 cup butter
1 cup sugar, granulated
1 egg
1 tsp. vanilla
1 1/2 cups flour, all purpose
1 tsp. baking powder
1/2 tsp. salt

Broiled topping
1/4 cup butter
1/2 cup brown sugar, packed
1/4 cup light cream
3/4 cup coconut, shredded, or use half coconut and half chopped nuts

Pour water over dates and baking soda; let stand until lukewarm. In bowl, cream butter with sugar; beat in egg and vanilla. Mix together flour, baking powder, and salt; add to creamed mixture alternately with date mixture. Spread in a greased and floured 9-inch square cake pan. Bake in 350°F oven for 40 minutes or until tester comes out clean. Broiled Topping: In a small heavy saucepan, combine butter, packed brown sugar, light cream and coconut (or coconut/nut mixture). Bring to a boil, stirring; boil gently for 1 minute. Spread over warm baked cake; broil until bubbly and lightly browned, watching carefully.[187]

PLUM TART

1 cup sugar

1/2 cup butter

1 cup flour, sifted

1 tsp. baking powder

2 eggs, well beaten

12 purple (Italian) plums, halved and pitted

1 tsp. cinnamon, or more, to taste

sugar

lemon juice

pinch of salt

Cream butter and sugar until light. Add flour, baking powder, salt, and eggs. Spoon the batter into a greased 9 inch springform pan. Cover the top of the batter with the plum halves, skin side up. Sprinkle well with cinnamon, a little sugar, and lemon juice. Bake at 350F for about an hour. Remove from oven and cool before serving plain or with whipped cream or ice cream.[189]

We reassure the reader that despite the stress of being accused of and tried (well, sort of) for a heinous crime against the Royal Couple, the Knave of Hearts' vital organ of the same name is still flourishing; we supply a diagram with the principal components labeled.[188] The knave's crime can easily be understood, though, especially if a delicious tart like this one was involved!

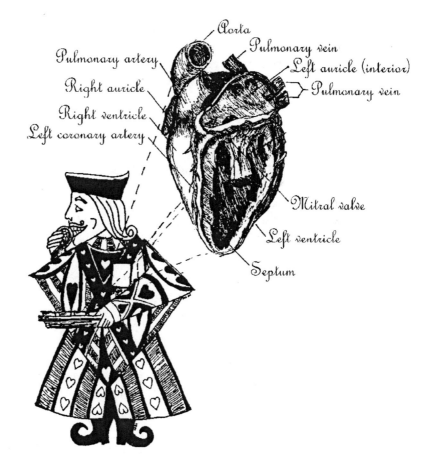

Aorta

Pulmonary artery

Pulmonary vein

Right auricle

Left auricle (interior)

Pulmonary vein

Right ventricle

Left coronary artery

Mitral valve

Left ventricle

Septum

SOTELTIES AND WARNERS

Sotelties originated in medieval times. They were sculptures or scenes made from edible ingredients and incorporated into elegant dinners as decoration or entertainment. Some could even be considered works of art or of scientific ingenuity. (The nursery rhyme about the singing blackbirds baked in a pie is a soteltie from a medieval feast.) However, as Alice knew, such preparations were not always intended to be eaten, nor were they necessarily safe to eat! (Sotelties should not be confused with "warners," which are disguised foods, such as marzipan fruit.)[190]

Almonds have been cultivated in the Middle East and Mediterranean areas for thousands of years. The Book of Genesis mentions (Chapter 43, Verse 11), that almonds were among the items to be delivered to Joseph (one of the sons of Jacob) while he was in the service of the Pharaoh. One of the most widely used forms of almonds is marzipan, a thick, moldable paste made primarily of ground almonds and sugar. Marzipan can be flavored, colored, rolled, and/or formed into various decorative shapes that are often life-like and/or elaborate. Marzipan items are usually painted in detail with food coloring, and may be glazed to preserve the finish.

Although this almond confection appeared in the Middle East as early as the fifth century, the name for it dates back only to thirteenth-century Persia. One putative origin is the name of the ancient Burmese city of Martaban, which was famous for the glazed jars that it exported, filled with preserves and sweetmeats. Another source may have been the Italian *marzapane*, from the Latin *massa*, for pastry, and *panem*, for bread. The word has been passed down, with a variety of intermediate spellings (e.g., marzepaine, marcipan, marzopane, marchpane), to the present day.

The first Europeans to taste this confection were probably the Crusaders, when they invaded the lands of Islam. A French knight wrote to his wife: "Never had I imagined that from such a simple base of ground almonds would it be possible to devise such a delicacy. The inhabitants of these lands are not as primitive as we have been told, for surely no barbarian could invent such a culinary marvel."[191] Travelers carried the recipe from one city to another, and marzipan became so popular that at least fifteen countries claim its invention; among them are Spain, France, Italy, India, and Japan. Many cultures enjoy this confection, both at special holidays and during the year.

Other, more recent and more obscure, meanings for "marzipan" (which have nothing to do with Alice or this cookbook!) include the filler used to patch automotive bodies, and, as "the marzipan layer" of business firms such as banks; i.e., the segment of bright younger people just below the partners. Neither of these has anything to do with this cookbook.

marzipan

2 cups sugar
2 cups blanched almonds, very finely ground
1 1/2 tbs. lemon juice
2 egg whites, beaten stiff

In a heavy saucepan, over a medium flame, heat the sugar and 1 1/4 cups of water, stirring constantly. When the mixture begins to bubble at the edges, add several drops of the lemon juice. Continue cooking and stirring until the mixture become syrupy. Reduce the flame, add the ground almonds and continue stirring until the mixture forms a ball the consistency of soft dough. Stir in the remaining lemon juice and, when well blended, remove from the heat.

Fold the stiff egg whites into the dough. Allow to cool for 15 to 20 minutes, stirring occasionally. Roll out the dough to about 3/4 inch thickness. Cut the marzipan into cookie, fruit or vegetable shapes. Place on a cookie sheet and let stand, uncovered, overnight to dry. To color the marzipan, brush lightly with a mixture of several drops of vegetable coloring dissolved in water after the cookies are dry.

To glaze the cookies (optional), beat together 1 egg white and 1/2 cup of confectioners' sugar until the mixture is white, creamy and thickened. Add 1 tsp. of lemon juice and beat another 5 minutes. Dip the top of each candy or cookie in the glaze and leave it on the cookie sheet until the glaze hardens. Serve fresh or store in completely dry, sealed containers.[192]

ANIMALS = MEALS

There may be an abstruse (and possibly circular, or more likely, square) mathematical explanation, grounded in surds and the absurd, for the reappearance of the animals that Alice had consumed during the course of this cookbook adventure.

Given that the dishes Alice prepared and ate consisted primarily of the animals in the story, and that the dishes she ate reasonably constituted "meals," we may set "animals" equal to "meals:"

$$animals = meals$$

Because this "proof" is merely theoretical, we need not use the actual number of the animals supposedly eaten, nor calculate the total number of meals we think Alice consumed in the preceding eleven chapters (although *she* certainly would know!).

Now, if the meals Alice ate can be considered "square meals" (and we think readers will agree that that was the case for most chapters of this work), the terms on both sides of the equation can be squared, giving us the following:

$$(animals)^2 = (meals)^2$$

However, we know that the meals were *eaten*, and thus no longer exist, so we must apply a negative sign to the "meals" term:

$$(animals)^2 = -(meals)^2$$

Now, if we want to analyze what happened to the animals, we may, quite properly, take the square root of both sides of the equation, to get us back to the original, unsquared term, "animals":

$$\sqrt{(animals)^2} = \sqrt{(-meals)^2},$$

or,

$$animals = \sqrt{(-meals)^2}.$$

However, there is no rational number that can be squared to yield a negative number; the square root of a negative number is irrational. The right-hand term, the surd, cannot be further reduced to a sensible quantity, and thus, we may reasonably conclude that it is all *absurd*, and entertain the possibility that the animals were *not* actually eaten, and could very well still be alive and healthy, just as Alice observed.

With the so-called trial over, Alice was tired and hungry, and longed for some nice tarts, and perhaps a nice selection of other tasty cakes! As she hastily ran home to get some dessert, she tripped over a large root in the path, and was very surprised to find *"herself lying on the bank, with her head in the lap of her sister, who was gently brushing away some dead leaves that had fluttered down from the trees upon her face.*

'Wake up, Alice dear!' said her sister; 'Why, what a long sleep you've had!'

'Oh, I've had such a curious dream!' said Alice, and she told her sister, as well as she could remember them, all these strange Adventures of hers that you have just been reading about," and about all the delicious and interesting recipes she had tried along the way.

How Alice felt at the end of this cookbook adventure! [193]

APPENDIX

Conversion table for American oven temperatures and British oven settings.

Temperature, F	Gas Mark setting
150	1/4
175	1/4
200	1/2
225	1/2
250	1
275	1
300	2
325	3
350	4
375	5
400	6
425	7
450	8
475	8
500	9
525	9
550	9

GLOSSARY

alembic – an apparatus consisting of two vessels connected by a tube, historically used for distilling liquids.

Alice – a small English girl, age 10, not suitable for use in any dish. Usually depicted with a blue ribbon in her long blond hair, and dressed in blue with a white pinafore. However, dress and hair ribbon color vary with illustrator.

bain marie – a pan of water into which a smaller pan can be set to cook food slowly, without burning, or to keep food warm.

betaine – any neutral chemical compound with a positively charged cationic functional group which bears no hydrogen atom and has a negatively charged functional group such as a carboxylate group which may not be adjacent to the cationic site. In biological systems, many betaines serve as organic osmolytes, substances that protect cells against osmotic stress, drought, high salinity or high temperature. Intracellular accumulation of betaines permits water retention in cells, thus protecting from the effects of dehydration. Dietary sources of betaine include beets, broccoli, and spinach. Interestingly, many wines contain betaine, particularly less expensive wines that use beet sugar to increase the alcohol content. Some experts suggest that this may be part of the so-called "French paradox," in which wine drinkers from France tend to have low rates of heart disease despite diets high in fat and cholesterol. Here is the chemical formula for trimethylglycine, the first betaine discovered: $C_5H_{11}NO_2$.

bouquet – (see bouquet garni).

bouquet garni – "garnished" bouquet, i.e., a combination of bay leaves, fennel, thyme and parsley; onions optional (as they usually are, except in French onion soup).

bubble and squeak – a traditional English dish made with pan-fried leftover vegetables, most often, potatoes and cabbage, but carrots, peas, Brussels sprouts, and other vegetables can be added. It is traditionally served with cold meat from the Sunday roast, and pickles. Theories as to the origin of its name vary, but it most likely comes from the sounds it makes while being cooked. Makes a nice accompaniment to toad-in-the-hole (see below).

callaloo – 1. a leafy, green vegetable that may vary by culture; in Jamaica, it is an amaranth, but in other places, it may be taro or a species of *Xanthosoma* (also known as coco, tannia, or dasheen bush). Outside of the Caribbean, water spinach is occasionally used. 2. the dish (a stew) made with callaloo. Not to be confused with "Callooh!" – an often chortled exclamation, but that's for another cookbook adventure.

callipée – glutinous meat of the under part of a turtle, mock or otherwise; undershell, or plastron.

case knife – a sharp kitchen knife kept in a "case" or sheath, the kind of knife with which Alice would have cut her finger had she not been such a prudent little girl.

caster sugar – caster (or castor) sugar is the British name of a very fine type of sugar, so named because the grains are small enough to fit though a sugar "caster" or sprinkler. (It is sold as "superfine" sugar in the United States.) Because of its fineness, it dissolves more quickly than regular white sugar, and so is especially useful in meringues and cold liquids. It is not as fine as confectioner's sugar. If you don't have any caster sugar on hand, you can make your own by grinding ordinary granulated sugar for a couple of minutes in a food processor.

cowan – a colloquial name for the alligator snapping turtle (*Macroclemys temminkii*), which is protected in all states except Louisiana, where they are prized for soup.

croquette – a French word for kromeskis.

defrutum – a 50% reduction of grape juice (or "must;" freshly squeezed grapes) used by cooks in ancient Rome. Pliny the Elder recommended that defrutum be boiled only at the time of the new moon, while Cato the Censor suggested that only the sweetest possible must should be used. (Duh!) As the use of bronze or copper kettles would give the finished product an unpleasant metallic taste, the preferred vessels for boiling and storing defrutum were made of, or were lined with, lead. (Given what we know today about lead poisoning, this was probably not a good idea!) The sweetest defrutum was further boiled down into a concentrate called sapa. The main culinary use of defrutum was to sweeten wine, but it was also added to fruit and meat dishes as a sweetening and souring agent and even given to food animals such as suckling pig and duck to improve the taste of their flesh. Defrutum was mixed with garum to make oenogarum, one of Rome's most popular condiments. Defrutum was often used as a food preservative, and some Roman women used defrutum or sapa as a cosmetic, which lent a truly sappy look to their otherwise plain faces.

diatoms – any of many primarily unicellular eukaryotic algae, one of the most common types of phytoplankton, which serves as the main food source for many larger aquatic organisms. They are encased within a unique cell wall made of silica (hydrated silicon dioxide) called a frustule. These frustules show a wide diversity in form, some quite beautiful and ornate. Fossil evidence suggests that they originated during, or before, the early Jurassic Period.

dram – a unit of weight in the U.S. Customary System equal to 1/16 of an ounce, or 27.34 grains; a little bit.

duodo – Portuguese word for a simpleton, like the authors of this book.

elevenses – the hour before twelveses, usually celebrated by consuming a few tasteless cookies called biscuits and coffee fortified with chicory to the point of being nearly unpotable, on the whole a British middle-class ritual not out of place in this Wonderland cookbook.

flamingo – a bright pink, long-necked, long-legged tropical bird prized in the ancient world for its succulent tongue, a dish in more recent times more often found on the menu of restaurants in Florida than Oxford.

flaps – the parts of a mushroom other than the stem (not to be confused with flap jacks or other less than edible flaps). Pickering [194] notes that: "The thin Filament is that to which the Edges of the Head of the Mushroom adhere, while it is what is commonly called a Button, and from which it separates by expanding to a Flap."

forcemeat – finely ground meat, fish, or poultry that is either served alone or used as stuffing.

garum – standard fermented fish sauce found in every kitchen, an ancient Roman delicacy which can also be used as a medicine for sick horses.

gaufre – a thin biscuit baked or, preferably, fried, in gaufre molds.

gentlemen's relish – a type of anchovy paste also known as *patum peperium*, supposedly created in 1828 by an Englishman named John Osborn. It tastes very strong, very salty and slightly fishy. It contains anchovies (minimum 60%), butter, herbs and spices. The exact recipe has remained a secret and has been passed down by word of mouth. The traditional way of eating Gentlemen's Relish is on thin slices of buttered white bread toast, either on its own, or with cucumber, or mustard and cress.

groats – hulled, and usually crushed, grain, primarily oats—not to be confused with the British four-pence coin of much denser consistency.

hing – asafoetida (*Ferula assafoetida*); also known as devil's dung, stinking gum, asant, food of the gods, ingua, hilteet, and giant fennel. It is an herbaceous perennial plant growing to six feet tall, with stout, hollow, somewhat succulent stems. The leaves are large and pinnately compound; the flowers are yellow. Asafoetida has a pungent garlic smell when raw, but in cooked dishes, it delivers a smooth flavor reminiscent of leeks. (See also silphium.)

hotchi-witchi – the classic English Gypsy hedgehog dish, indescribably delicious except in Romany.

jar – a jug, as in jugged hare (see jug). Not to be confused with *nightjar*, a medium-sized, insectivorous, nocturnal bird with long wings, short legs and a very short bill, sometimes referred to as a "goatsucker" from the mistaken belief that it sucks milk from goats. (It does not!)

jug – a tall earthenware crock, into which a hare was placed for cooking (see also, pipkin).

kromeskis – a Polish term for croquette.

lagomorphs – the family of mammals that includes the rabbit and the hare. The two prominent front teeth of rabbits and their relatives might lead one to assume that they are rodents (another group with two prominent front teeth), but, as readers of this cookbook have learned, appearances are deceiving. The chewing teeth of rabbits and hares, as well as various other anatomical factors, assign them to a taxonomic family of their own.

mace – an aromatic spice made from the dried, waxy, scarlet or yellowish covering that partially encloses the kernel of the nutmeg. (Not to be confused with the medieval weapon used to bludgeon one's enemies.)

magirologist (also, **magirist**) – an expert cook; from the Greek word for "cook." (What the authors of this book are not!)

magirology – the art or science of cooking.

mesentery – the folded sheet of peritoneum in which the jejunum and ileum are suspended from the dorsal abdominal wall; the embryonic precursor of these structures, a double layer of splanchnic mesoderm attached to both the dorsal and ventral walls of the body, which also temporarily supports the organs of the chest.

molasses – dark syrup; the American term for treacle.

oenogarum – a mixture of defrutum and garum.

omentum – a fold of the peritoneum connecting the stomach with the liver, spleen, colon, etc. (Watch out for the etc.!) [Clearly a Latin word but one whose origin is yet to be unfolded.]

orangerie – a sheltered, brightly lit structure similar to a greenhouse; used for the cultivation of citrus fruit in colder climates.

paunch – usually, a noun meaning *stomach*, or *belly*; but, in this case, a verb meaning "to remove the entrails of." Appropriate in cookbooks but not to be used in polite society.

parboil – to boil the par out of something, hence to boil thoroughly.

peckish – inclined to peck, with the nose, not a very helpful hunger-alleviating activity, unless one is a member of the taxonomic order *Aves*.

peptides – a chain of amino acids, the building blocks of animal proteins, which are essential to this cookbook.

Peter Pan – a brand of American peanut butter named after a dubious character in another well-known children's book and of absolutely no relevance to these pages.

pettitoes – usually, the feet of a pig, sometimes called pig's trotters, but can also refer to the feet of a child or small ape, neither of which is recommended as an ingredient for the recipes of *this* cookbook.

pipkin – a jug; a small earthenware or metal vessel or cooking pot. (Not to be confused with a ramekin.)

pudding – 1. a sweet dessert containing flour or other cereal product that has been boiled, baked, or steamed. 2. a sausage-like preparation made with minced meat, blood, or other animal products, often stuffed into a bag or skin, and boiled.

puff paste – puff pastry; a light, flaky dough that is formed by rolling and folding the buttered dough in layers so that it expands when baked.

quince – 1. the hard, apple-like fruit of a western Asian shrub, *Cydonia oblonga*; usually cooked in order to be considered edible. 2. the Spanish word for the number fifteen, which is certainly not as important to readers of this book as the number forty-two!

quenelles – another French word, this one meaning: forcemeat of different kinds, composed of fish, poultry or meat, eggs, etc., shaped in various forms (balls, ovals, dodecahedra, etc.), poached and served as an entrée or a garnish for soup.

ramekin – a small, glazed, heatproof ceramic dish, most commonly round or oblong, in which a single portion of food is both cooked and served. (Not to be confused with pipkin.)

ramequin – French form of ramekin.

rue – 1. a genus of strongly scented small evergreen shrubs in the family Rutaceae, native to the Mediterranean region, Macronesia, and southwest Asia. The plant has feathery compound leaves and yellow flowers. Rue was used extensively in Middle Eastern cuisine in olden days, as well as in many ancient Roman recipes (according to Apicius), but it is very bitter, and not much used now. 2. what readers might do if/when they try these recipes.

sapa –   a concentrated form of defrutum.

scone – probably derives from the Hamburg dialect word "Schönroggen," referring to a seedcake with two acute and two obtuse angles; but now, alas, an all but generic wheat or barley cake baked on a griddle and cut into quadrants or wedges, usually served with orange marmalade or jam and clotted cream.

secretagogue – a substance which causes another substance to be secreted; has nothing whatsoever to do with secrets.

sendal – a thin, light silk used in the Middle Ages for fine garments, church vestments, and banners.

silphium – a plant of the genus *Ferula*; generally considered to be an extinct, giant fennel that once formed the crux of trade from the ancient city of Cyrene for its use as a rich seasoning and as a medicine. The valuable product was the resin (*laser, laserpicium,* or *lasarpicium*) of the plant. It was harvested in a manner similar to asafoetida, a plant with similar enough qualities to silphium that Romans used the same word to describe both. (See also hing.)

sippets – little bits of toasted or fried bread, often served with soup, broth, meat, or ice cream.

stirabout – an Irish word for the Scottish porridge, not to be confused with other stirabouts.

toad-in-the-hole – a main dish that consists of sausages (the "toads") baked within a pan of dough (the "hole"), a savory complement to bubble and squeak. But, as neither appear in the story proper, that's all there is to that.

treacle – dark syrup, British word for molasses, best drawn from wells.

urticant – any substance that causes itching or an itchy rash; derived from the botanical name of the stinging nettle, *Urtica dioica*. Anyone who has run into a stinging nettle can appreciate the meaning!

Vitamin C – ascorbic acid, a micronutrient necessary for human life, thought by many, quite incorrectly, we scarcely need add, to have been invented by Linus Pauling.

white stock – stock refers to the broth in which meat, fish, poultry, vegetables, or bones are simmered for a long period; this is used as a base in preparing sauces, soups, and gravies. To keep the stock "white," no blood or other pigmented materials are added.

zest – 1. the thin outer peel of citrus fruits. 2. a quality with which Alice sought and prepared her recipes.

References

1. Electronically altered from frontispiece in *Mrs. Beeton and her Husband, by her great niece*. Nancy Spain. London: Collins, 1948.

2. Rumpolt, M. *Ein new Kochbuch* : das ist: ein grundtliche beschreibung wie man recht und wol, nicht allein von vierfüssigen, heymischen und wilden Thieren, sondern auch von mancherley Vögel und Federwildpret, darzu von allem grünen und dürren Fischwerck, allerley Speiss ... kochen u. zubereiten solle .. durch Marxen Rumpolt ; [hrsg. u. mit e. Nachw. vers. von Manfred Lemmer]. 2. Aufl., Neudr. [d. Ausg. Frankfurt am Main, Feyerabends, 1581]. Leipzig : Edition Leipzig, 1977, title page illustration.

3. Engraving of orange, Harter, J., Ed. *Food and Drink. A Pictorial Archive from Nineteenth-Century Sources.* New York: Dover Publications, 1979, p. 92.

4. Reynolds, D. *The Daily News*, Jan. 29, 2003.

5. http://www.lothene.demon.co.uk/crafts10.html.

6. Reynolds, D. *The Daily News*, Jan. 29, 2003.

7. http://www.lothene.demon.co.uk/crafts10.html.

8. Turner, E., ed. *The Color Book of Pressure Cooking.* London: Octopus Books Ltd., 1978, p. 86.

9. Farmer, F.M. *The Boston Cooking School Cookbook*, Boston: Little, Brown, and Co., 1915, p. 576.

10. Marmite™ logo, http://www.brandsoftheworld.com/countries/uk/107477.html

11. http://www.gty.org/~phil/marmite.htm#whatis.

12. http://www.worldhealthcare.net/marmite/his6.html.

13. The authors are indebted to Edward Wakeling for their knowledge of marmite soldiers, and for the directions for their construction.

14. http://www.crfg.org/pubs/ff/currants.html.

15. Photoscan of commercial packaging for SunMaid (brand) Currants.

16. http://www.wholehealthmd.com/refshelf/foods_view/1,1523,67,00.html.

17. http://www.raisins.org/history.html.

18. http://www.foodreference.com/html/fraisins.html.

19. Crane, E.W., personal communication, 1987.

20. Source unknown; all rights, where applicable, are retained by the owner of the image.

21. British Farm Council and British Tourist Authority. British Cookery. Croom Helm Ltd., 1977.

22. Wilson, K.G. *The Columbia Guide to Standard American English*. NY: Columbia University Press, 1993.

23. Bradley, M. *The British Housewife*. London: S. Crowder and H. Woodgate, 1756, pp. 560–561.

24. Ibid., p. 561.

25. Ibid.

26. Ibid.

27. Adapted from a recipe posted by "Bright" at http://www.globalgourmet.com/kitmailrecs/KM0986.html.

28. Engraving of rabbit, Hart, H.H., Ed. *The Great Giant Swipe Book*. New York: Hart Publishing Co., 1978, p. 262.

29. U.S.D.A. Circular #540.

30. Text and diagram, Graham, P.G., Price, M.S., and Marriott, N.G. Virginia Cooperative Extension Service, Publication #454878, June 1998.

31. Beeton, I. *Mrs. Beeton's Victorian Cookbook*. Topsfield, MA: Salem House Publishers, 1988, p. 109. (Originally published in 1861 as *Beeton's Book of Household Management*.)

32. Hartley, D. *Food in England*. London: MacDonald, 1964, p. 176.

33. Keating, S. *The Times*. London, July 26, 2003, p. 60.

34. Pliny. *Historia Naturalis* with English translation by H. Rackham. Cambridge: Harvard University Press, 1983, pp. 376–378.

35. Text and photo, http://www.dodopad.com/dodofact/dodofact.htm

36. Friedmann, H. New light on the dodo and its illustrators. In: Annual Report of the Board of Regents of the Smithsonian Institution, Washington, D.C., 1955; Hachisuka, M. *The Dodo and Kindred Birds*. London: H. F. and G. Witherby, Ltd., 1953, pp. 49–85; http://news.nationalgeographic.com/.

37. Engraving of dodo, O'Shea, M.V., Ed. *The World Book Encyclopedia*, Vol. 4. Chicago: W.F. Quarrie and Co., 1917, p. 1986.

38. http://www.dodopad.com/dodofact/dodofact.htm

39. Pöppig, E. *A German Menagerie Being a Folio Collection of 1100 Illustrations of Mammals and Birds*. 1841; http://www.davidreilly.com/dodo/gallery.html

40. http://www.dodopad.com/dodofact/dodofact.htm

41. http://news.nationalgeographic.com

42. www.davidreilly.com/; http://www.dodopad.com/dodofact/dodofact.htm; http://www.amnh.org/

43. Shapiro, B., Sibthorpe, D., Rambout, A., Austin, J., Wragg, G.M., Bininda-Edwards, O.R.P., Lee, P.L.M., and Cooper, A. flight of the dodo. *Science 295*: 1683, 2002.

44. Duck image, Hart, p. 355.

45. 38. TurDuckEn was originally conceived by Paul Prudhomme in the 1980s.

46. Gillon, E.V., Jr., Ed. *Picture Sourcebook for Collage and Decoupage*. New York: Dover Publications, 1974, p. 32.

47. Engraving of blue crab, Hart, p. 284.

48. http://www.tpwd.state.tx.us/fish/specinfo/crab/crabbro.htm; http://water.dnr.state.sc.us/marine/pub/seascience/bluecrab.html

49. http://www.blue-crab.net/

50. Ibid.

51. Ibid.

52. Schwabe, C.W. *Unmentionable Cuisine*. Charlottesville, VA: University of Virginia Press, 1979, p. 225.

53. Farmer, p. 318.

54. Hearn, P.L.T.C. *La Cuisine Creole: A Collection of Recipes from Leading Chefs and Noted Housewives, Who Have Made New Orleans Famous for its Cuisine.* New Orleans: F.F. Hansell and Bro., Ltd., 1885, p. 31.

55. Engraving of oyster, Hart, p. 284

56. Engraving of oysters on piling, Ibid., p. 285

57. http://www.edsrestaurant.com/embarcad/emoyst.html); http://www.edsrestaurant.com/embarcad/emoyst.html): http://www.cuisinenet.com/digest/ingred/oyster/nat_hist.shtml; http://www.ballylongford.com/ballylongfordoysters.htm; http://www.manandmollusc.net/molluscan_food_files/molluscan_food_5.html.

58. http://www.freerecipe.org/Main_Dish/Seafood/Oysters/spindled-oysters-recipe-gmfr.htm.

59. Leslie, E. *Directions for Cookery, in its Various Branches*. 10th Ed. Philadelphia: E. L. Carey and Hunt, 1851, p. 59.

60. Ibid., p. 57.

61. Marcus, G. and Marcus, N. *Forbidden Fruits and Forgotten Vegetables*. NY: St. Martin's Press, 1982, p.124.

62. Hart, p. 339.

63. http://www.uga.edu/vegetable/cucumber.html

64. A.C.T., family recipe.

65. Iguana meat was, at one time, available from Mercadito Ramos II, in Langley Park, MD, and at Todos Hispanic Supermarket in Woodbridge, VA.

66. Recipe modified from one shown on Food Network, 2002.

67. Engraving of gila monster, Hart, p. 269.

68. Doyle, M.E., and Egan, J.M. Glucagon-like peptide-1. Recent Progress in Hormone Research 56: 377-399, 2001; Meier, J.J., Gallwitz, B., and Nauck, M.A. Glucagon-like peptide-1 and gastric inhibitory polypeptide: potential applications in type 2 diabetes mellitus. *Biodrugs* 17: 93–102, 2003.

69. http://www.earthfirstjournal.org/efj/feature. cfm?ID=115&issue=v22n2.

70. The Food Insects Newsletter, Vol. 4, 1991; http:// www.taa.org.uk/TAAScotland/EdibleCaterpillars2. htmwww.fao.org/Gender/en/foreb2-e.htm; http:// www.food-insects.com/book7_31/Chapter%2017%20 ZAMBIA.htm; http://athena.english.vt.edu/~hbrizee/110 6coloniallinksfarming.htm.

71. http://www.food-insects.com/book7_31/Chapter%20 17%20ZAMBIA.htm.

72. Photo of caterpillar, Gillon, p. 9.

73. Latham, P. http://www.taa.org.uk/TAAScotland/ EdibleCaterpillars2.htm; http://www.food-insects.com/ book7_31/Chapter%2017%20ZAMBIA.htm.

74. http://www.food-insects.com/book7_31/Chapter%20 17%20ZAMBIA.htm.

75. Ibid.

76. Ibid.

77. Ibid.

78. http://www.earthfirstjournal.org/efj/feature. cfm?ID=115&issue=v22n2.

79. Schwabe, p. 370.

80. Ibid.

81. Ibid., p. 371.

82. Ibid., p. 373.

83. Ibid, p. 374.

84. Gordon, D.G. *The Eat-a-Bug Cookbook*. Berkeley: Ten Speed Press, 1998, p. 69.

85. Yack, J., Smith, M.L., and Weatherhead, P.J. Caterpillar talk: acoustically mediated territoriality in larval Lepidoptera. Proceedings of the National Academy of Science (USA) 98: 11371–11375, 2001.

86. http://www.conservation.state.mo.us/nathis/ mushrooms/.

87. Engraving of mushrooms, Gillon, p. 25.

88. http://www.greennature.com/article1989.html.

89. http://ohioline.osu.edu/hyg-fact/3000/3303. html);http://www.ces.ncsu.edu/depts/pp/notes/ General_Principles/gpin004/gpin004.htm.

90. Smith, W.G. Mental effects of fungus poisoning. *The Graphic*, 15 November 1873.

91. http://www.botany.hawaii.edu/faculty/wong/Bot430/ Lect24_Edible%20and%-20Poisonous%20Mushroom. htm.

92. Beeton, p.117.

93. Ibid., p.72.

94. Guggisberg, R. *Cooking with an African Flavor*. Nairobi: Mount Kenya Sundries, Ltd., 1993, p.11.

95. Hoffmann, W.E. Insects as human food. *Proceedings of the Entomological Society of Washington* 49: 233, 1947.

96. http://www.geocities.com/fyrdup67byrd/history. html; http://www.tipplers.com/nepal/facts.htm

97. Beeton, p. 103.

98. Jefferson, T. *Artificiall Embellishments*. Oxford: William Hall, 1665. *In The Housewife's Rich Cabinet*, by Jean Miller, Francie Owens, and Rachael Doggett. Washington, D.C.: The Folger Shakespeare Library, 1997, p. 116.

99. Engraving of pig, Harter, J., Ed. *Food and Drink. A Pictorial Archive from Nineteenth-Century Sources*. New York: Dover Publications, 1979, p. 85.

100. National Swine Registry, West Lafayette, IN.

101. National Pork Board (U.S.A.).

102. National Pork Board (U.S.A.); New Zealand Pork Industry Board.

103. Engraving of pig with meat-cut code numbers, Harter, J., Ed. *Food and Drink. A Pictorial Archive from Nineteenth-Century Sources.* New York: Dover Publications, 1979, p. 85.

104. Beeton, p. 91.

105. Schwabe, p. 83.

106. Ibid., p. 104.

107. Ibid., p. 117.

108. Ibid., p. 94.

109. Gilbert, R. *Moose Mousse and Other Exotic Recipes.* NY: Simon and Schuster, 1964, p. 30.

110. Brewer, E.C. *The Dictionary of Phrase and Fable.* Philadelphia: Henry Altemus, 1898, p. 691.

111. Beeton, p. 107.

112. Photo of treacle jar, http://www.goodnessdirect.co.uk/cgi-local/frameset/detail/586901_Rayners_Organic_Black_Treacle_340g.html

113. http://www.ochef.com/316.htm.

114. http://www.wymsey.co.uk/wymsey/treacle.htm.

115. Hughes, J.T. "St Margaret's well at Binsey near Oxford: the treacle well of Alice in Wonderland". *Pharmaceutical Historian*, 34: 54–58, 2004.

116. Ibid.

117. Ibid.

118. Ibid.

119. http://www.plotka.com/plotka/issure10/treacle.htm.

120. http://bread.allrecipes.com/AZ/BlckTrclScns.asp.

121. Garmey, J. *Great British Cooking: A Well Kept Secret.* NY: Random House, 1981, p. 182.

122. http://greatbritishkitchen.co.uk/gbk/recipes/desserts/treaclepudding.htm.

123. Galizia, A. and H.C. *Recipes from Malta.* Valetta, Malta: Progress Press Co., Ltd., 1979, p. 58.

124. Harrison, V., Administration Officer, The Mammal Society, 15 Cloisters House, 8 Battersea Park Road, London, SW8 4BG; www.mammal.org.uk.

125. An earlier version of this text, with the recipe, appeared in *Bandersnatch*, Issue 11, April, 2001.

126. http://www.olddormouse.net/6733.html?*session*id*key*=*session*id*val*

127. Ibid.

128. Engraving of roses, Harter, J., Ed. *Harter's Picture Archive for Collage and Illustration.* New York: Dover Publications, 1978, p. 68.

129. http://pages.prodigy.com/gardenshop/roseherb.htm.

130. http://www.jungleroses.com/recipe.html.

131. Ibid.

132. Ibid.

133. C. Plini Secundi. *Naturalis Historiae*, libri XXVII. Carolus Mayhoff. Stuttgart: B.G. Teubner, 1977.

134. Shackleton Bailey, D.R. [ed.] *Martial. Epigrams.* Loeb Classical Library. Cambridge: Harvard University Press, 1993, p. 200.

135. Vehling, J.D. Apicius. *Cookery and Dining in Imperial Rome.* A bibliography, critical review, and translation of the ancient book known as *Apicius de re Coquinaria.* NY: Dover Publications, Inc., 1977, p. 230.

136. *Suetonius.* Edited by J.C. Rolfe. Loeb Classical Library, Vol. 2. London: William Heinemann, 1930, p. 266.

137. *Scriptores Historiae Augustae.* translated by David Magie. Loeb Classical Library, Vol. 2. London: William Heinemann, 1924, p.146.

138. Douglass, J. "The Natural History of the Phoenicopterus or Flamingo, with two Views of the Head, and three of the Tongue of that beautiful and uncommon Bird." *The Philosophical Transactions of the Royal Society of London*, 1716, No. 350 reprinted in *The Philosophical Transactions of the Royal Society of London*, from their Commencement, in 1665, to the year 1800. Edited by Charles Hutton, George Shaw, and Richard Pearson. London: C.&R. Baldwin, 1809, plate vii., pp. 268–271.

139. Thompson, D.W. *A Glossary of Greek Birds.* London: Oxford University Press, 1936, p. 305.

140. *National Wildlife Magazine*, Feb.–March, 1982, inside of front cover.

141. Pichon, Jérome, ed. Le Ménagier De Paris, *Traité De Morale Et D'économie Domestique Composé Vers*, 1393; also see text on flamingoes.

142. *The New York Times*, March 30, 2002.

143. http://en.wikipedia.org/wiki/Countershading; http://www.africanconservation.org/dcforum/DCForumID16/8.html

144. http://www.lincolnzoo.org/; http://www.dublinzoo.ie/.

145. Petulengro, G. *A Romany Life.* New York: 1936, E.P. Dutton and Co., pp.78–79.

146. Blerbert, J.-P. *The Gypsies.* Translated by Charles Duff. NY: E. P. Dutton and Co., 1963, p.186.

147. Borrow, G.H. The Zincali, *An Account of the Gypsies of Spain.* London and Toronto: J.M. Dent and Sons, 1924, pp. 61-62.

148. Rumpolt, p. LXI.

149. Leland, C.G. *The English Gipsies and their Language.* London: Trubner and Co., 1874, pp. 203–204.

150. Smart, B.C. and H.T. Crofton. *The Dialect of the English Gypsies.* London: Asher and Co., 1875, p. 85.

151. Boretzky, N. and B. Igla. *Wörterbuch Romani-Deutsch-Englisch für den südosteuropäischen Raum.* Wiesbaden: Harrasowitz, 1994, p. 135.

152. Clare, J. *The Poems of the Middle Period, 1822–1837.* Vol. 5. Eric Robinson, Ed. Oxford: Clarendon Press, 1996, pp. 363–364.

153. Beeton, p. 155.

154. Hieatt, C.B., Hosington, B., and Butler, S. *Pleyn Delit: Medieval Cookery for Modern Cooks.* Toronto and Buffalo: University of Toronto Press, 1976.

155. Petulengro, G. *Romany Remedies and Recipes.* San Bernardino, CA: Borgo Press, 1980, p. 6.

156. *The New York Times*, March 18, 1900, p. 29.

157. Gordon, E. *The Life and Correspondence of William Buckland.* London: John Murray, 1894, pp. 104–105.

158. http://www.turtleman.com/turtle3.html; http://www.parcplace.org/education/sparc/trip25.htm.

159. McConnaughey, J. Associated Press, September 1, 2001 and September 10, 2001.

160. Roman, J. and Bowen, B. Stalking the mock turtle. *The New Scientist*, Sept. 8, 2001, p. 28.

161. Simon, A.L. *A Concise Encyclopedia of Gastronomy.* NY: Harcourt, Brace, and Co., 1954, pp. 459–460.

162. Schwabe, p. 87.

163. http://erazo.org/chefrick/recipes/mockturtle.htm.

164. Thewissen, J.G.M., Hussain, S.T., and Arif, M. Fossil evidence for the origin of aquatic locomotion in archaeocete whales. *Science 263*: 210–212, 1994.

165. Thewissen, J.G.M., S.I. Madar, and S.T. Hussain. Ambulocetus natans, an eocene cetacean (Mammalia) from Pakistan. Courier Forschungsinstitut Senckenberg 191: 1–86, 1996.

166. http://www.neoucom.edu/DEPTS/ANAT/Thewissen/

167. BBC Worldwide, Ltd.

168. Gee, H. *The Guardian*, London, Sept. 20, 2002, p.10.

169. Thewissen, J.G.M., S.T. Hussain, and M. Arif. Fossil evidence for the origin of aquatic locomotion in archaeocete whales. *Science 263*: 210–212, 1994.

170. Venning, C. In: *The Listener*, Vol. 59, No. 1505, Jan. 30, 1958.

171. Boles, L.C. and Lohmann, K.J. True navigation and magnetic maps in spiny lobsters. *Nature 421*: 60–63, 2003.

172. Rumpolt, p. CXXVI.

173. http://penelope.uchicago.edu/Thayer/E/Gazetteer/Places/Europe/Italy/Umbria/Perugia/Bevagna/Bevagna/Roman/baths/mosaic.html

174. White, J. *Lobster at Home*. NY: Scribner, 1998, p.170.

175. http://earth.leeds.ac.uk/~jackson/shoal/w.html; http://www.edinformatics.com/culinaryarts/food_encyclopedia/whiting.htm

176. A.C.T.

177. Engraving of fish, Hart, p. 159.

178. Beeton, recipe and photograph, p. 49.

179. Image of pepper package, Harter, J., Ed. *Food and Drink. A Pictorial Archive from Nineteenth-Century Sources*. New York: Dover Publications, 1979, p. 93.

180. http://www.colonialspice.co.uk/; http://www.uni-graz.at/~katzer/engl/.

181. http://www.uni-graz.at/~katzer/engl/.

182. Adapted from Krochmal, C. and A. *The West Indies Cookbook*. Albuquerque, NM: Border Books, 1992, p. 44.

183. http://www.geocities.com/Wellesley/7510/kingcake.html; http://nutrias.org/~nopl/facts/kingcake.htm.

184. http://www.geocities.com/Wellesley/7510/kingcake.html.

185. http://www.floras-hideout.com/recipes/recipes.php?page=recipes&data=q-r/Queen_Elizabeth_Cake, from: Ferguson, C. and Fraser. M. *A Century of Canadian Home Cooking 1900 through the '90s*. Scarborough, Ontario: Prentice Hall Canada, Inc.

186. http://www.freerecipe.org/Dessert/Baked_Goods/Cakes/queen-cake-recipe-bscr.htm.

187. http://www.floras-hideout.com/recipes/recipes.php?page=recipes&data=q-r/Queen_Elizabeth_Cake, from: Ferguson, C. and Fraser. M. *A Century of Canadian Home Cooking 1900 through the '90s*. Scarborough, Ontario: Prentice Hall Canada, Inc.

188. Diagram of heart anatomy adapted by A.E.K. Carr from *Gray, H. Anatomy, Descriptive and Surgical*. Ed. by T.P. Pick and T. Howden. NY: Bounty Books, 1977, p. 466.

189. Crane, E.W., personal communication, October 22, 1986.

190. http://www.kingdomofacre.org/food.html; http://www.florilegium.org/files/FOOD-SWEETS/sotelties-msg.text; http://www.foreverwed1.com/articles/themes/024554n.html

191. http://www.stratsplace.com/rogov/israel/marzipan_madness.htm.

192. Ibid.

193. Illustration electronically altered from the original by John Tenniel, in: Carroll, L. *Alice's Adventures in Wonderland*. London: Macmillan and Co., 1865, p. 188.

194. Pickering, R. "A letter from the Reverend Mr. Roger Pickering, V.D.M. to Cromwell Mortimer, M.D., R.S. Secr. [i.e., Secretary of the Royal Society] concerning the seeds of mushrooms." *Philosophical Transactions*, Vol. 42. (1742–1743) London: Royal Society, p. 598.

Afterword

Various literary interpretations have been proposed concerning Lewis Carroll's intentions regarding the edibility of the animals in his *Alice's Adventures in Wonderland*, and of Alice's appetite. For interested readers, we present short excerpts from two of these as "food for thought" (and also because they help to justify the overall concept of this "cookbook"!).

From Nancy Armstrong (*Fiction in the Age of Photography*. Cambridge, MA: Harvard University Press, 1999, pp. 221–223):

"...the dangers contained in Alice's body begin and end with her mouth".

"Carroll saw to it that Alice would have a problem controlling her mouth, when he gave her a prodigious appetite and put her in a world made of food."

"Alice's situation...invites us to consider why Carroll animated a world by bringing the copious modern dinner table back to life, and why he had his heroine acquire her identity in relation to objects so strangely revitalized."

From Daniel Bivona (*Desire and Contradiction: Imperial visions and domestic debates in Victorian literature*. Manchester and NY: Manchester University Press, 1990, p. 65.):

"...it is not surprising that the beings about which they discourse all seem to be creatures whose 'animal' existence is but prelude to their ultimate end as meals; they can be 'understood' as 'essentially meals.' "

"The mere fact that 'eating' or 'being eaten' appears to be the telos of most of the creatures discussed suggests that events in Wonderland have assumed a distinctively oral 'Alician' cast..."

"...to define animals teleologically as meat for the table is but a thin disguise for a process which 'recentres' Alice at the end of the chain of nourishment; for in Alice's universe, meals ultimately exist for the purpose of being eaten by human beings like herself."

[Authors' note: This might be an instance of the Great Chain of Nourishment theory in the history of ideas.]

index

LaVergne, TN USA
12 May 2010
182503LV00003B/47/P